Dear Mary Kay -
What a lovely "chance meeting"
Enjoy!   Albert

1/6/2011

A Brooklyn Odyssey

Travails And Joys Of A Boy's Early Life

Albert Rothman

A BROOKLYN ODYSSEY — Travails and Joys of a Boy's Early Life
Copyright © by Albert Rothman, 2008

Printed in the United States of America

Published by WingSpan Press, Livermore, CA

www.wingspanpress.com

The WingSpan name, logo and colophon are the trademarks of WingSpan Publishing.

First Edition 2008

ISBN 978-1-59594-281-4

Library of Congress Control Number: 2008938237

FOREWORD

Where is the end of childhood? Certainly not in the sixth grade, nor the eighth grade, nor the high school years. No, we retain childhood as adults, hidden, perhaps, but willing to emerge when we open to it and think as a child.

CONTENTS

Toyland, toyland,
Little girl and boyland.
While you dwell within it you are ever happy then.
Childhood's joyland, mystic merry toyland.
Once you pass its borders, you can never return again.

> From Victor Herbert's "Babes in Toyland."
> Words by Glen MacDonough.

BROOKLYN is a place of many lands and a boy may have many childhoods there.

Albert at age 1.5

I. BEGINNINGS

Who can remember our beginning? We start in mother's womb, but what follows is lost in time's womb.

Records show that I emerged from a human cocoon on January 16, 1924. "The Night of January Sixteenth" was a long running play in New York almost ten years later. I would have loved to pretend that it was in celebration of my birthday!

Like an archeologist, I mine my mind, trying to remember the past, often with sparse results. Some memories are like little traces that pop up and then fade. Winken, Blinken, and Nod steal into my mind, from over seventy years ago. In my imagination I see three men in a boat, like a washtub floating in the sky. They have stars on their blue caps. The recollection may have come from a children's book from my past. My mind's ear hears my old Victrola, scratching out the words and music to "Jack and Jill went up the hill to fetch a pail of water."

Memories began to clear at age four when I developed a taste for danger. I copied other kids and taunted an older boy. "Hey, fat Solly!" He ran after us. I was the smallest and the one he caught. He hit me. I ran crying to my mother.

"Why do you call him names when you know he'll hit you?" Mother said. I had no response. It was fun to stick my tongue out, tease him and run away, like the other kids. The temptation was strong. So I continued to tease Solly, and he continued to hit me. On our last clash he tore open my thumb on a picket fence. That cured my addiction to the masochistic game. The injury left an indentation on my right knuckle. Even now I can see a faint sign of the injury.

Older boys often took apart two-part roller skates to build a scooter, improvised from an orange crate on a two by four. The front two wheels were the front half of the skate, the back two the heel part. The scooter wheels were sounds I heard:

STORM

Whirlwind
       howling in the street—
       sucking up
regurgitating
street dusts
that scratch my eyes.

Leaves
chase one another
in angry circles.

Gray clouds nestled in black
race across the sky, prelude
 to a summer storm
 ready to burst
 accompanied by raspy sounds—
 skate wheels
on rough sidewalks.

Years later a storm brings back
       spinning clouds
       and hollow wind
of childhood's memory.

Even a painting—
ominous skies
of El Greco's Toledo
recalls the impending storm
and the scraping of skate wheels
on Brooklyn streets.

TONSILLECTOMY

"Where are we going, Mom."

"We have to go to a hospital, so you won't get so many sore throats," she said.

"What will they do in the hospital?"

"They'll fix you, and you will feel better," Mother said.

"Will it hurt?" I said.

"The doctor won't hurt you, and you'll get lots of ice cream."

I'm suspicious. If it won't hurt, why is Mother promising me ice cream?

"I don't want to go to the hospital!" But we did go there.

The medicine smell in the hospital scared me. I screamed, "I want to go home!" The nurse grabbed me, laid me on a table covered with a white sheet and held me down.

The doctor came in smiling and said, "We'll give you ether that will make you sleep, and you won't feel any pain."

I was scared even more. *Pain? What will they do to me while I'm sleeping?*

They put a box or something over my face. I yelled some more.

"You're a smart boy. I know you can count. Now just count backward from 100," the doctor said.

I was crying, but I began to count, one hundred, ninety-nine. "I can't breathe. I'm choking!"

Later I awoke. I didn't like the smell of ether all around me. I almost threw up. My throat felt like it was filled with pebbles. Every time I swallowed, the pebbles rubbed against my throat. *What did they do to me, and why did they lie?* "Mommy! My throat hurts awful."

She sat by my bed and touched my arm. "I'm here, Albert. You're all right," she said. "The sore throat will go away soon."

I didn't believe her after what they told me. "Where's the ice cream you promised me?" This time it was the truth. I got vanilla. It even hurt to swallow the ice cream, but the coolness

Mother and Dad near Grant's Tomb in Manhattan

smoothed everything so I didn't hurt as much. I had more ice cream than I ever had in my life. At home I got even more. After I get better, Mother didn't give me a lot more. But my throat didn't hurt, either.

SCHRAGGS

They were family friends. Mr. Schragg drove a laundry truck and let us ride with him. Usually we traveled by bus or on the subway. We never owned a car.

Those laundry trucks were wide, with a spacious front seat. Mother and Dad sat in the passenger seat. I sat on Dad's lap. This was well before seat belts were required.

A car entered from a side street and collided with us. Nobody was hurt, but I bumped into the windshield. My forehead was bruised and red. Mother insisted that we proceed to a hospital.

I yelled, "No! I won't go to a hospital!" I remembered what they did to me when they removed my tonsils. I won this time. Since I wasn't badly hurt, why did they want me to go to the hospital?

The answer approach was, "If possible, sue!" a typical New Yorker's attitude. In The Depression years, money was scarce and lawyers much cheaper than today. A money settlement would help put food on our table.

Afterwards, Mother shook her head and scowled. She said that we lost the opportunity to collect for the accident. I didn't care. I would have kept kicking and screaming before I'd go to a hospital.

OFF TO SCHOOL

I was five and beginning a long school journey. Public School (PS) 159 was only the beginning. Six months in kindergarten and off to PS 64, 197, 100, 158, 179, then to junior high school and high school. I feel out of breath, just remembering! I grasshoppered too fast.

I attended my second kindergarten in a different school. We moved to the lower floor of a two-story home owned by Uncle Harry and Aunt Adele, who lived above us. The house was on Vermont Street in the East New York section of Brooklyn. Nearby were New Lots Avenue and the elevated train tracks of the IRT (Interborough Rapid Transit), an old subway company in New York City.

ELEVATED TRAIN

The wheels screech
I look up, listen, see
the dark train in the black night
its lights intermittently dimming
as the train arcs the elevated track.
The scene and sound indelible
in my mind.

Years later creaking sounds
remind me of that track.
Even a line of car headlights
curving down a distant grade
returns me to the time
when I was five.

EARLY HORROR

A first born, I longed for an older brother. One of my first substitutes was Yosl Kitrosser, a few years older, but young enough to be a playmate. Years later I learned that the Kitrossers were my second cousins, related to my father. *Yosl* is Yiddish for Joseph.

In the way my mind bounces around, I remember a Yiddish song at the time. "Oy oy oy Yosl, Yosl, Yosl, Yosl", that was translated into "Yinglish," (part English, part Yiddish) and became a popular song.

We adopted a long alley behind a string of houses as a play yard. Although cars could drive along this dirt way, there were so few cars that we were safe.

Yosl and another boy were throwing darts toward a tree. The boy missed his target and a dart stuck in Yosl's leg. He yelled in pain. I was shocked when I saw the sharp point embed in his leg. Blood droplets formed and dripped to the ground. He wasn't seriously hurt, but I was horrified by the thought of a body being penetrated. Recalling the event made me close my eyes and shudder.

Six or seven years later a neighborhood boy climbed up on a garage roof and jumped down. His arm tore open as he landed on barbed wire. I felt faint with a mixture of nausea, repulsion, and fear when I heard his screams and saw the blood spurt and the entrails of his arm displayed as in a medical textbook. I was upset by my first look into the makings of a body. It could have been my body.

TREATS

Late one afternoon I was warmed by the sun shining through the gauzy curtains before Dad was to come home from work. He brought me a kaleidoscope that entertained me for hours. I loved turning the toy tube and was fascinated by the constant forming and reforming of the patterns. Even as an adult, I remain intrigued and charmed by the changing vision when I rotate the tube. The child lives!

Dad often brought home three boxes from Loft's Candy Shop in Manhattan. They had a special sale, three for a dollar or perhaps it was fifty cents. One box contained chocolate-covered candy, another chewy caramels. Cashews were in the third box. Mother doled out the candy and nuts to me. She knew I wouldn't voluntarily stop *fressing*, the Yiddish word for eating rapidly, gorging.

I still relish chocolates (who doesn't?) and cashews. Now

I assume Mother's role and put them away after a few pieces to prevent myself from devouring them endlessly, from *fressing.*

OLD WIVES' MEDICINES

Mustard plasters on the chest, vinegar on the forehead, enemas in the rear, and on and on. Where did these home-grown treatments come from? Who started them, and why did they continue?

As a child, if I had a chest cold, out would come dry mustard mixed with water to make a mustard plaster. This hell-and-brimstone melange was placed in a cloth and plopped on my suffering chest. I felt as though it would burn a hole in me. Could this miserable practice have derived from ancient devil-worship?

My mother suffered from constipation. Stewed prunes accompanied her breakfast. I recall the frequent pained look on her face that reflected the agony of the resistant bowel. Of course I never observed her bathroom habits, but I suspect that enemas frequently accompanied her to the toilet. "What goes around comes around." Sixty years later, constipation stalks me. In my case it's caused by medications, but the effect is the same. I no longer scoff at Mother's affliction.

When I was sick, out would come the hated rubber bag with its red snake-like tube and an evil-looking black mouth, the torture dispenser. I had to lie down while she inserted this twentieth-century version of the medieval rack into a very personal part of my anatomy. The penetration was painful.

"More Vaseline, Mom!" Holding the bag high, she clicked the valve open, and Old Faithful began to parboil my intestines. I yelled, "too hot!"

She squirted some of the water on her wrist and pronounced, "It's not too hot," my gut's sense notwithstanding. The execrable fluid poured into me until I felt as though my insides would burst. Again I hollered an objection. She delayed a bit and then poured on more, as though the beast would not be satisfied until she had allowed it to void completely.

She admonished me not to release the water. I felt as though the fluid would erupt before I could reach the toilet. I barely made it in time. She told me to hold it in, but the liquid oozed out in spite of my efforts. After a lifetime, she gave me the OK to let it out slowly. I longed for relief. When she turned away, I let the liquid out as rapidly as I dared, until I felt less pressure in my belly. At last I allowed a slow release.

How could an enema possibly affect the course of a disease? The prospect of the threatened procedure made me hide symptoms that might call for the red bag.

When I had a sore throat, she gave me hot water with lemons and sugar, that did seem to alleviate the soreness for a while.

The cures seemed worse than the diseases. Perhaps the unexpected consequence of the treatments was to make me heal faster, to rid myself of those torments.

Mustard plasters for chest cough, alcohol rubdown for fever, and enemas for mother's anal fastidiousness. Also, I was fed vitamin D as cod liver oil, the lubricious bane of children. I somehow survived those old wives' remedies.

BATH

I was a wavy-haired child. When my hair dried after a bath, every strand went its own unresolved direction. To deal with this problem, mother placed part of an old stocking on my wet head before bed. Next morning my hair was plastered down. The waves had sunk into my scalp.

VIOLIN LESSONS

Poor immigrant Jews often had their little boys learn to play the violin. Did this come about because violins were easy to carry when Jews were ousted from their homes in Europe?

Perhaps. Pianos took up much more space and were less transportable, even in Brooklyn. Since my family moved so often from one apartment house to another, large instruments were out of the question. The initial cost of a piano, high enough compared to a violin, would have been multiplied if the family moved frequently, and especially if the move was above the first floor. I have seen pianos moved up apartment house stairways, or through outside windows after being hauled on the outside of apartment buildings. But violins were for us.

When I was five years old I wanted to play the violin. Or so my mother later maintained. Mr. Smilowitz, my violin teacher, played in the Paramount Theater orchestra in Brooklyn. Orchestras were common in larger theaters. He came halfway across Brooklyn by streetcar to give me a weekly lesson. For this he received one dollar, from which he assumed the cost of a roundtrip that cost a dime. My part of the bargain was to practice an hour each day. Therein lay the rub. I preferred to play outside instead of consorting with the violin. For a while I barely cooperated but rarely gave in without a fight. Smilowitz thought I had talent and wanted to bring me to his maestro at the Paramount.

It was not to be. After a year and a half of continual battles, Mother finally gave up. My parents could hardly afford a dollar a week during the Great Depression, especially since I refused to cooperate.

Do I regret giving up the violin? Most certainly! Although I no longer took lessons, I didn't abandon the instrument entirely. Several years later we moved to the flat above Grandma. I played Jewish melodies squeakily that my grandma loved— "Eli-Eli" and "Hatikvoh." Squeaky or not, her grandson's playing delighted Grandma.

Much later I played second violin in the junior high school orchestra. I hated the "mm,uh uh, mm,uh uh" of the second violin part, instead of the melody line that the first violins were blessed with. In high school I played second violin for a while. That was enough to quell any desire to play further, at least for then.

As an adult I took violin lessons along with my son. We played duets together, much more satisfying than my previous violin experiences. Sometimes when we played a Bach Concerto for two violins, laughter accompanied us as we got out of sync.

Sometime later I played in the local symphony, once again the second violin part that I disliked. More pleasurable were duets with a friend who played cello. With him I had an opportunity to sing a melody line on my violin.

Eventually I abandoned the violin because of other pursuits. Lonely and resentful, it sits in a deserted corner of my living room.

MANHATTAN BEACH "EXPOSED"

There were some advantages of being a child of five. Brighton Beach was a public shore for hoi polloi. Aunt Sina, whose husband was well-to-do, had a membership in the fenced-in private Manhattan beach nearby. She brought Mother and me there. Because of my age, I accompanied them to the women's side of the dressing areas. Although I pretended not to look, my eyes surreptitiously enveloped women's bodies, especially their breasts, as we walked through the area. It was an early inkling of future desires.

II. FIRST GRADE

As if in a Conestoga wagon, my parents moved again to a different Brooklyn neighborhood. I was in my third school, while still in first grade. The kids seemed to know one other in my class at PS 197. I knew none of them. How was I supposed to fit in?

The pretty girl whose dark hair hung down in long curls seemed to like Sam. I wished she would choose me as partner in the class games, or even look at me. What was so special about Sam? He was just as short as me, and wore glasses. I didn't.

I thought of Pearl when went to bed at night. I was in love, but I had to keep it a secret. If she didn't like me, I'd die if she knew I liked her, if all the kids knew I liked her. They'd tease me.

Sometimes I chose her as a partner, but only sometimes. If I chose her all the time, the kids would guess how I felt. But Pearl always chose Sam. It didn't seem fair!

On the way to school I had to cross Ocean Avenue, a broad thoroughfare at the corner of Avenue O where we lived. There were few cars at the time and so crossing wasn't too dangerous. But Mother watched closely when I crossed the avenue. She trusted me to cross the smaller Avenue O by myself to buy groceries for her or to visit Uncle Lou. His house was next door to the store.

MILK OR ICE CREAM

A small A&P store was on the corner, across the street from our house. Large supermarkets and major chain stores had not yet arrived. This was not a "serve yourself" store. I waited my turn. With a broad smile, a grocery clerk took the requested items from the shelf or refrigerator. He removed the pencil tucked behind his ear, licked the lead point and totaled the prices on a brown paper bag.

Mother sent me to buy a bottle of milk. My thoughts were on ice cream. How I would love to eat a chocolate-covered vanilla pop! I imagined biting into the rich chocolate and letting the smooth vanilla slide down my tongue and throat. She handed me the milk-money and I obediently crossed Avenue O, still musing about ice cream. After waiting to be served, I made the purchase. I crossed the street and returned home. Mother was waiting.

She asked, "Where is the milk?"

I was happily licking ice cream. "Milk?" I had completely forgotten why I was sent to the store. I told her I didn't mean to use the money for ice cream—I wasn't thinking about the milk. Mother laughed and said she understood. She gave me money to go back and get the milk.

It was my first experience that unconscious desire could overcome one's conscious demands.

But that ice cream tasted so good!

GLASS IS SO FRAGILE

I was home from school on a Jewish holiday. Nothing interesting to do and no friends to play with since I am new in this neighborhood. But I was resourceful. I picked up a large rock and bounced it on the sidewalk several times. I was intrigued by the unexpected directions it took, not at all like a ball. I wondered where the rock would go next, maybe a budding scientist's curiosity. The glass door of the apartment house was adorned with black metal scrolls. Uh-oh! The rock bounced its own way, and ignoring the presence of the metal, crashed through the plate glass door.

My parents couldn't afford the cost of a new glass door. Fortunately, the landlord covered the loss from insurance, perjuring himself that the breakage occurred from person or persons unknown.

One would think that even a seven-year-old would learn from his mistakes, but not I. Trouble followed me, or more likely, I followed trouble.

One of my favorite twelve-year-old cousins, Morty, was like an older brother. I looked up to him and was happy that he was visiting. While Aunt Sarah and Mother were talking in the kitchen, Morty and I had a pillow fight in the living room. After a few skirmishes, my cousin heaved a pillow at me. My quick reflexes came into play. I ducked. Unfortunately I was standing in front of the window. Even more unfortunately it was closed. Pillows are soft, but windows are fragile. Crash! At least I wasn't the one who did the damage, even though I was an accomplice. The landlord's insurance paid for the damage once more. We must have had an understanding landlord, or else he had adequate insurance and claimed a passing stranger did the deed.

I wonder why my parents moved so often. I don't think it was related to my glassy escapades. Or was it?

Cousins Dick, Morty and Albert in front
of an unbroken window

Cousin Sidney and Albert

INTRODUCTION TO SEX

My introduction to sex took place innocently in the backyard and basement of our apartment house. Toby was a girl I played with. In the usual experiments that children do, we decided to explore one another's genitals. I had never seen a girl nude, and so I suggested to Toby that she could see my penis if I could see her vagina, that we called our wee-wees. We descended the few steps to the basement for privacy, realizing that grownups would disapprove of our experiment. I was fascinated by her lack of a penis and the smoothness and simplicity of the region between her legs. I touched her there. She was interested in my appendage, although somewhat less than I was in her lack of one.

Uh-oh! Her older cousin Leonard surprised us. He threatened to tell our mothers. I don't think he did. At least I didn't remember any repercussions.

EDDY

I was five and a half when Eddy was born into our family. I didn't want a younger brother. Besides, he drew too much attention to himself. He had so many earaches that Mother spent much of her time taking care of him. I saw her only at meals, when the only attention I received was criticism.

SHELDON

"Leave him alone, Sheldon!" I said, in warning.

Sheldon, a bullnecked boy with close-cropped dark hair was teasing Eddy, my kid brother. I almost inadvertently wrote "bother." He was a bother.

Eddy was my nemesis, through no fault of his own. But he was also my private victim for teasing, scaring, and whatever sadistic activity that might escape parental detection. To be fair to myself, there was a more positive side to my behavior. I taught my brother songs like, "I like mountain music, good ole mountain music, played by a real hillbilly band…" I was kind to him as he (and I) got older, and often I was his advisor.

I was in the courtyard of our apartment house. My friend Sheldon was bothering Eddy, who began to cry. I shouted, "Stop it!" Almost without thinking, my hand reached out for an orange crate, one of the props we used for constructing forts. The box, as if by an unseen force, descended on Sheldon's head. I was surprised and alarmed to see an oozing red pool drowning the short dark fur on his head. I wondered who had wielded the box. Then I realized that I had.

Years later when I read Camus' *l'Etranger*, I felt a terrible recognition. When I hit Sheldon I had been moved with the same impulse as that of Camus' character, Mersault, who had been moved by a force beyond himself. Mersault didn't even feel as though he was the actor when he murdered.

I, however, immediately felt the guilt of my act. Mothers descended on the scene. Their faces white with horror, they applied towels and washcloths. Probably Sheldon was hurried off to the doctor. I didn't remember.

I retreated, waiting for the inevitable. I wandered to the school playground and then circled the block a few times, using up the remaining hours left before dinner. I slinked into the apartment to hear, "How could you do such a thing? Hitting a child on the head with a weapon? What's the matter with you?"

A weapon? I used a weak defense even I didn't believe— protection of my brother.

"Sheldon's father is very upset and is coming down to talk to you." I was an animal trapped within these walls. My panic led me to a clothes closet, where I huddled, sobbing quietly, hoping I was adequately hidden. The dark was comforting, until a spear of light penetrated. I was revealed!

Mr. Gottlieb pointed to Sheldon's bandaged head and asked me quietly why I hit his son. In a halting hollow voice, I tried to explain about my brother.

Through my tears I said, "I'm sorry. I didn't mean to hurt Sheldon."

Inside I knew, but couldn't seem to put in words my surprise that I had hit him, my fear when I saw the blood flow, my deep guilt, the anticipated fear of Sheldon's father. But all those feelings remained my unexpressed secrets.

Gently he said, "You shouldn't ever do such a thing again."

I took a deep breath, relieved. Sheldon's wound was minor, and we remained friends.

ARTIST ABNER

I drew airplanes and copies of the Dick Tracy cartoon character. I owned a stamping print set and made my own newspaper. But neither drawing nor journalism would become my calling.

In 1932, Franklin Roosevelt was elected President. My classmate, Abner, made what seemed to me a masterpiece—-a cartoon of a prizefight, in which a referee was raising the arm of a victorious Roosevelt. Former President Hoover who lost the election was lying flat on the canvas. Perhaps Abner copied the drawing from a newspaper, but when I saw the craftsmanship of his sketch, I decided that I had no drawing talent, and abandoned any pretense as an artist.

In my middle age I took a class and found that I could draw fairly well, after all.

ENCHANTED BY RADIO LADIES

When I was seven, some radio programs enchanted me. A regular feature was *The Lady Next Door.* Her sweet voice told stories that kept me spellbound. Years later I learned from *The Encyclopedia of American Radio* that her name was Madge Tucker.

As an adult I heard the music that had introduced the *Lady Next Door.* The tune was a transition from one piece to another on a classical music station in San Francisco. Excitedly I phoned the station the next morning. The woman who answered my SOS immediately identified it as "The Musical Box," also known as "The Musical Snuff Box," composed by the Russian, Liadov. I was delighted to retrieve a connection to a childhood memory.

Another of my heroines was *The Kellogg Singing Lady*, on the air Saturdays. I used to listen raptly. She had a gentle quality that my mother lacked, when she criticized me. Some years later I found a recording of the Singing Lady in the Museum of Radio in Manhattan, and learned that her name was Irene Wicker. There was no mention of the theme song that introduced her half-hour. I can whistle the tune, but I don't know its name. I'm still searching. Someday I expect to jump up excitedly when I hear that song on the radio.

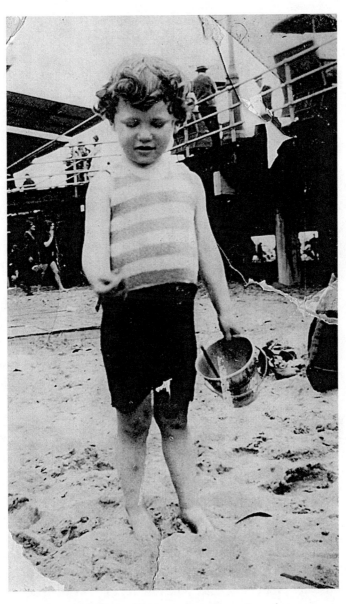

Sandboy Albert at Brighton Beach

III. BRIGHTON BEACH

On sunny weekend mornings, my family boarded the BMT (Brooklyn-Manhattan Transit) Coney Island Express train, and sat together on the woven cane benches. The subway car rocked its way to the Brighton Beach station where the underground tracks surfaced to an elevated platform. We walked a few blocks to our lockers, located in the backyard of a one-story house. My family rented the locker for the summer season. A group of these lockers surrounded an open shower. We changed to our bathing suits, stored our clothes, then headed to the beach.

Years later when I open the drain of my sink, I smell a dank, almost fetid odor that reminds me of the scent rising from the shower drain in the backyard. I assume it was mold.

The word locker reminds me of a Mel Brooks recording, *The Two Thousand Year Old Man.* Carl Reiner, interviewing him, asked if he spent time in Europe. The ancient man responded with an exaggerated Yiddish accent, " Europe? I had a locker dere," a response that brought laughter to anyone who grew up knowing the beach milieu. Jewish humor with an edge of irony. When I tell this story to others, they ask me, "What is the joke?" The joke is the comparison of Brighton Beach lockers with where tourists might stay while visiting Europe. Of course, like any joke, to explain it is to miss the point.

After a morning of swimming and lying on the beach, we walked a few blocks to Coney Island Avenue for an inexpensive Chinese lunch, perhaps fifty cents or less. I wince now when I remember that we called it "the Chink's." It wasn't intended to be prejudicial, but merely an insensitive short cut, in common use at the time. I would of course never use that word now. After lunch we returned to the beach. I was banished from swimming for an hour or two, "while your meal settles, otherwise you could drown." Mother's warning and prohibition.

Ride'm, Cowboy!

At the end of day, we returned to our locker, showered to wash off the sand and dressed for the trip home. Our faces and arms glowed, tender from the day's sunburn.

Supper in the evening consisted of some, if not all of the following—corned beef, salami, garlicky Kosher hot dogs, Heinz vegetarian baked beans, smoked whitefish and carp, pickled herring, sour pickles, fresh sauerkraut, rye bread and bagels—a delicatessen feast, in short. We washed it all down with cream soda or seltzer from a pressured bottle with a spigot. The bottles were delivered to our door.

MOVING TO BRIGHTON

A moving van was in front of our apartment house. Once again I had to leave my friends, or more accurately my acquaintances. There hadn't been enough time to make close friendships. I spent the past year trying to learn the rules of how to behave with other boys and girls. Each school had new games, new teachers, new rules. Even the schoolyards were different. I felt lost, and lived in my own cocoon, that protected me from the frightening world. There was usually a girl to fall in love with, to dream about, to want to walk hand-in-hand with, to feel special with. But I was always too frightened to tell her. And most often she had a boy she chose for the year or two before this newcomer appeared.

My mother thought it would be healthier for us to live near the ocean, and so we moved to Brighton Beach. We rented the lower floor of a bungalow on Sixth Street. I listened to Bob Hope on the radio in the days before he became famous. He sang "Blue Moon," and a parody of the song, "I Surrender, Dear," that became "My Suspenders, Dear." One of the roomers named Ries often teased me. A joke he told me was, "Have you heard the latest news?" His answer: "It hasn't come out yet." Much later I've tried this on others, but most either don't get it or don't think it's funny. Maybe they are both right.

A naked man exited from the outdoor shower in our courtyard and headed toward his locker. Mother saw him from the window, and he smiled and waved at her. Mother cited this to convince me that being seen naked was not something to be upset about. Mother's argument did little to convince me. I thought I'd rather die than be seen naked by a girl.

Since I was a newcomer to the street, a group of boys invited me to play hide and seek. I was delighted to be accepted so readily. After covering my eyes and counting to one hundred, I went looking for them. After a long search, I finally gave up and went home. I learned that this was a standard trick played on a newcomer.

A good thing about this place. I slept in a screened-in porch. From there I could look out and see the fireworks from the beach at night. Since then I have always delighted in firework displays on the Fourth of July.

Gone were PS 159, 64, and 197. I entered the second grade at PS 100. I became a stranger again, where all the kids knew one another from the first grade.

NEMESIS IRVING

Irving was my new nemesis. He must have been his mother's darling, his platinum air in wild fluffs of curls. But only the fluffs were wild. Irving was a conformist, a goody two-shoes. I imagined that he was treasured by constituted authority and was the teacher's pet. Even his lisp must have endeared him to aunts and little pinafored girls. Next to him I felt like a gross young bull in a china shop, though lacking the strength of the animal. Seeing Irving for the first time I felt resentment, jealousy, and a deepened sense of loneliness.

The children were still talking about the recent class play that I missed. Irving had played the role of George Washington. Irving's hair could have been created from paintings of our first president.

The fall evenings lengthened. Halloween drew near. In the season we would chalk the sidewalks, a grand city tradition that predated graffiti. Multicolored chalks were available in the candy store, but they cost a few pennies that we preferred to hoard. Store chalk was soft and wore out quickly on the rough sidewalks. So like the other kids I helped myself to the hard school chalk that didn't wear down so easily. Also unlike the soft type it didn't stick to clothes, so there were fewer complaints at home.

Called to the blackboard in class, I wrote out a sentence. I reached out for two sticks of chalk, surreptitiously pocketing one of them. I wrote with the other. While my right hand continued to write, my left hand slithered to the ledge and more swag filed my pocket. I felt smug, rich, and ready to attack the sidewalk with my artistry.

"Miss O, Albert stole chalks and put them in his pocket." Irving, the little bastard had watched from his seat while the teacher was looking elsewhere. I felt panic.

There was no escape when the teacher commanded, "Albert, empty your pockets." This thief was caught with a smoking gun. At that moment, my rejection by a rule-making adult world far outweighed any identification with the rule-breaking, peer world. Shame, embarrassment, despair, and guilt crowded each other so rapidly, that I felt only hollowness. I wished the ground would open and swallow—me, the teacher, the chalk, and Irving.

The teacher plucked the stolen items from my reluctant, outstretched hand. "I will keep these here in my desk drawer and show them to your parents when they visit during Open School Week."

Witch, torturer! What worse punishment could she have possibly dreamed up?

She had instinctively located my jugular.

Every night I agonized before falling asleep. The fear of

being exposed as a thief to Mother and Uncle Abe, my judges. I imagined hearing, "Albert, stealing! I never would have thought that of you. What happened to that good boy?"

What good boy? Only a good-boy mask. I knew what a bad boy I really was. In later years I likened myself to Calvin in my favorite comic strip "Calvin and Hobbes." Even the fantasy of beating up Irving couldn't compensate for exposing my secret—the bad boy hidden inside me.

My dread grew as the dark days lengthened. I slept little the night before the beginning of Open School Week. The imagined monsters grew larger in my dark bedroom, finally frightening me into troubled sleep.

Morning. The day dragged on, so slowly.

Suddenly the time came. Mother and Dad visited my classroom. I remained at home, waiting for the axe to fall when they returned later that evening. Nothing. Just, "How come you're still awake?" Then the usual criticisms from mother, but not a word about my felony. I inhaled deeply. Was it possible? Once again I had narrowly escaped ignominy. Yet I was left with a sense of regret. I didn't beat up Irving with the full force of my fury. In truth, I didn't even approach and beat him up at all.

A small outbuilding in the schoolyard had separate toilets for boys and girls. One day as I was relieving myself, a woman brought her little boy in to, in my mother's words, "do his duty." We boys were outraged by this incursion into the sanctity of male territory, but what could we do about a thoughtless adult?

FRIEND ELMER

We moved within a year to a flat in a house on Second Street, still in Brighton. This time I didn't have to change schools.

I formed a relationship-in-mischief with Elmer. I had much to learn from him. Curly-haired, with a cherubic face that belied mischievousness, he was much more daring than I. We built fires in the empty lots, and roasted potatoes that were called *Mickeys*, that nowadays would be considered a non-politically-correct reference to the Irish.

MICKEYS

Potato scent
cooking in a microwave
returns me to mickeys—
potatoes roasting in a fire
on an empty city lot.

Half burned, half raw
stolen fruit
the aroma captured with the char
they burn our mouths
delicious, we pretend.
Two seven-year old
co-conspirators.

Mother doesn't allow fires.
     Allow?
These are our creations
our freedom from rules.
I stand downwind
or else my smoky smell would tattle
and I'd be scolded severely.
Smoke spirals
I spiral synchronously.
Fire wins
     smoke wins
     eyes smart.
My jacket is redolent with disobedience.

Elmer's family was fairly well–to-do, unlike mine. They even had a live-in maid. When the maid wasn't looking, Elmer swiped potatoes from the cupboard, but this time the maid was on guard.

"Follow me," Elmer said, like a sergeant at war. We went to Brighton Beach Avenue under the elevated train structure. Across the street was a greengrocer with outdoor bins. Elmer grabbed some potatoes as I waited nearby. The owner saw him and gave chase, but Elmer was a fast runner. Innocently I watched until they were out of sight. I went home and wondered whether he was caught. The next day he told me that he ran to the boardwalk, jumped down into the sand, and ditched the man.

I wonder whether he grew up to be a white collar criminal!

The time with Elmer was one of the most exciting and adventurous times of my early life. A large family of deaf mutes lived a few doors away from our house. The boys of the family bombarded with us with rocks, that we promptly hurled in return. Nobody got hurt, surprisingly, but the war waged on until we all were tired and went home.

Most of the people who lived in Brighton Beach were first or second generation Jews from Russia or other Eastern European countries. The elders spoke Yiddish, their *lingua franca*, to apply an incongruous metaphor. Many years later, a new generation of Russian Jewish immigrants populated the area.

Jews were persecuted in Czarist times and the years after. In post-Revolution Soviet Union, Jews experienced somewhat less official discrimination. As they integrated into Russian society, the Russian language mostly displaced Yiddish in their speech. Unlike their earlier countrymen in the US, the more recent immigrants spoke Russian, though many knew some Yiddish.

I visited ten years ago and found that Russian signs and food stores have filled Brighton Beach Avenue, so exotic, so different from the old Yiddish days.

REPORT CARD

Monday arrived. I sat at lunch facing my father, who was unemployed at the time, and so he was at home during the day. I felt uncomfortable with Mom, but it was worse with Dad looking on, because I hated to disappoint him.

Mother said, "Albert, is that your report card?"

"Yeah, Mom. Here. I got all A's in my work."

" Let me see." She looked it over carefully.

"Why do you have a C in conduct?" Mother said.

I didn't answer her, but Mrs. O doesn't like me, and I hate going to her class each day.

"You usually get a B in conduct, and that's bad enough, but now a C. Why can't you get an A. Was it for talking in class as usual?"

"I just can't help it. When I think about something, I like to talk to my friends about it."

Dad said firmly, but gently, "Son, can't you control yourself?"

I remained silent, but my answer would be, I suppose I could, and though I only half-realized it, I wouldn't. *I hate the teacher. She's mean and has a moose face.*

"You ought to keep quiet in class, if that's what your teacher wants."

Mother continued on my case. She sniffed my plaid Mackinaw. "Albert, you've been making fires again. I've told you many times, it's too dangerous. You could get burned."

"Aw, Mom, there's nothing else to do. Elmer and I just roast mickeys 'cause we like to make them ourselves. We won't get burned, and the potatoes taste so good."

"I cook potatoes at home, so there's no excuse to make fires." Mother just didn't understand the fun of making fires and eating our own mickeys.

"Where do you get the potatoes?"

I swallowed and lied. I told her that Elmer's mother gave

them to him. I didn't want to tell her that he took the potatoes from his house when his maid wasn't looking, and if he couldn't, he stole them.

Mother shrugged and made a face. "Do your homework, Albert."

I waved my hand in the air. "It's done already. It's easy."

"Are you sure you went over it carefully?"

"Yeah," I said to get Mom off my back.

"Then practice your violin." She pointed to the closet where the hated object was.

I'd rather go out and play. I picked up my violin, and made squeaky sounds by sliding my fingers up and down the strings, while bowing.

"That's not practicing. "Ambitious!" she said emphatically from the kitchen. Her other favorite criticism was, "Time-waster!" No wonder I tend to fill time, and rarely just relax, even though what I do is often inefficient and likely is unconscious time-wasting.

Another of her caustic expressions was the Yiddish, "*Es frehts mir zehr*," which means "It makes me very happy," sarcasm for "I couldn't care less." I often abbreviated it as FMZ. I hated sarcasm, but unaware sometimes I use it now. Some news stories on public radio give far more details than I want to hear. As a friend recently said to me, "I heard more from the lecture than I even wanted to know," certainly sarcasm.

Mother would sit at her Singer sewing machine and hum songs. Nearby was a red Sweet-Touch-Nee tin that originally held loose Chinese tea and later became a repository for clothes buttons. Her constant humming accompanied the humming of the Singer. I was annoyed almost as much as when I was a frequent captive listener when Mother tuned the Saturday opera on the radio, and I heard the screeching sopranos. Yet thanks to mother I enjoy the music of the early operettas and some light classics that she hummed and sang, including Waldteufel's

"Skaters' Waltz" and Strauss waltzes. I even attend some local classical opera performances—sopranos and all.

I reluctantly zipped through my violin lesson for ten boring minutes. I wanted to go outside to meet Elmer. We were expecting another fight with the kids next door. We planned to get even with them for the rocks they threw. This time we stored a bunch of rocks. The violin battle resumed. Mother kept nagging me, so I rushed through my violin lessons, and went outside.

An hour later, after another rock-throwing contest with the neighbor kids, I came back in. Mother was crying. "What's the matter, Mom?"

"We have no money and your father doesn't earn enough for us. I should have married a professional man and one who can speak English better."

I hated it when she criticized my dad and made me feel sorry for her. I took her side, and nodded my head. Then I felt angry. I loved my father. He was always kind to me and did all he could to earn a living. I didn't know why I made fun of his accent sometimes, but I felt sorry afterward. Mother admitted that he was a good man, and that made me even angrier. I didn't like to listen to her complaints. I was confused and upset.

That evening I turned on the radio, to hear the love lives of "Myrt and Marge," a soap opera.

I turned down the sound and put my ear close to the speaker. I didn't hear my mother's footsteps. She walked in from the kitchen to find me at the radio. "What kind of program is that for a boy? You should be ashamed, listening to love stories."

I felt ashamed and embarrassed. I hated my mother for shaming me. What was so wrong about listening to a love story? I especially hated it when she criticized me for not doing what she wanted. But what could I do about it?

I thought, "Leave me alone. I don't need you. And don't leave me. I need you." Years later I learned the word ambivalence.

Sunday night was family radio time. Eddie Cantor, Jack

Benny, and Colonel Bowes' Amateur Hour. On Eddie Cantor's program, young Bobby Breen sang his sweet soprano. My parents oohed and ahhed! I felt jealous. Why didn't they express pride in me? I'm not famous, but so what? I knew my father was proud of me, but I wasn't sure about Mother. I thought, "Gee, I'm the smartest kid in all my classes. Why doesn't she say she is proud of me for being a top student all the way through school."

Years later a cousin told me that that Mom was proud of me. I think she mistakenly believed that I would try harder and be more likely to succeed if she kept egging me on. Perhaps to get recognition from her, I strove to get top billing in grades throughout school years. I thought that was my claim to family fame. In some ways it was, but it didn't feel very satisfying.

Boys love to grow up, become men, and so we liked to take on their appurtenances, such as storm boots and air rifles.

STORM BOOTS

Leather storm boots
mine at last.
Calf length, they impel
my nine-year-old swagger.
The adornment—
leather pocket that snaps
shut.

I treasure
      the boot
      the knife
      the compartment
on the side of my boot
encasing the knife
and the snap securing it.

Looking back, I'm surprised, amazed that my parents allowed me to own an air rifle, a BB gun. How did I ever talk them into it? I've heard that some boys lost their sight from a shot in the eye. Perhaps they never heard that information. Lucky me. But I hardly remember using the gun. I wonder what ever happened to it? It's like one of my lost treasures.

DIXIE CUP LIDS AND TRADING CARDS

What riches we had in the nineteen-thirties! Dixie cups holding yin-yang patterns of luscious chocolate and vanilla ice cream. A bonus, if not the main reason, to buy Breyer's or Horton's were the cup covers that pictured movie stars, wild animals, circus performers and American Indians. Also Clark Gable, Myrna Loy, and James Cagney. And animals, the tapir with its strange snout, wildebeest, though I loved pronouncing both consonants in its alternate name, "gnu," and of course the King of the Jungle, mouth open as if growling at me. The circus snake-lady charmed me with her lovely, reptile-draped body covered with tattoos. Indians—Blackfoot Tribe warrior, standing tall in full feather and deerskin, and the cragged face of Sitting Bull with his jet-black hair pulled back in a ponytail.

My jaws were often sore from chewing the stiff flat pink rectangles coated with a sweet white powder. After chewing the bubble gum for minutes, the sweetness was gone, and the wad became a bore. Although the gum didn't have the smooth delight of ice cream, the cards that came with each packet were also great collectibles, featuring prominent baseball players like Honus Wagner, Babe Ruth and my special hero, Iron man Lou Gehrig, with his dimpled, smiling face.

We saved the cards and traded to fill out our holdings. We tried to win them from each other by flipping them to the ground, and calling the match, heads or tails. You could increase your collection that way, or even lose it all.

Popsicles of frozen, flavored water were treats. Chocolate-covered vanilla pops were even more delicious. On hot summer days the neighborhood man in a white truck came by, playing his Siren songs and selling ice cream. I often bought twinned orange popsicles that enclosed a vanilla center. Some sticks were imprinted with prizes to be claimed. I sucked a pop greedily to reach its wooden base. I could hardly wait to see if I had won a prize, though I never did. I wondered if anyone ever got a prize, but I continued to have faith.

All I had to show from the commercial past were a Little Orphan Annie secret decoder ring and a set of cards from the H-O Oats sponsored radio program, with sketches of Bobby Benson, Tex, Windy, and the H-Bar-O Ranch.

EXOTIC POSTAGE STAMPS

My aunt Ada's husband, Lester Rosenberg, was a tall, dark, handsome man. Maybe that's why he eventually found another woman and left Aunt Ada. Oh, she could be a know-it all, as I found out when I reached my teens. Before he left, he was Uncle Lester to me. He gave me foreign postage stamps from all over the world and a fat Scott Stamp Catalog to put them in. It had hundreds of pages with pictures of stamps. What a treasure! Vivid US stamps, like Whistler's Mother, Roger Williams, Christopher Columbus, and many others. And I was especially attracted to the Yosemite green stamp, the orange Grand Canyon stamp, and other colorful ones of the National Parks. I couldn't imagine that many years later I would actually visit and hike in those places.

There were head shots of our presidents. But the pictures of camels and yaks were much more interesting.

Foreign stamps, especially from countries I had never heard of made me daydream—Tannu Tuva, Togo, Tonga, but even ones that I had heard of like Italy, Finland, and Yugoslavia. I was intrigued that the spelling on the stamps *Italia, Suomi, and Jugoslavija* was different from what I had known. They conjured up distant places that were so far from my own experience in Brooklyn, and they sent stars of wonder to my eyes. The stamps were far more interesting than geography studies in school, where bored, I had to memorize what food each state grew. Who cared that Iowa grew corn and Kansas grew wheat? Or was it vice versa? But I was studious and felt I had to pass exams on these tiresome matters.

I enjoyed looking at it the triangle- and diamond-shaped stamps of Tannu Tuva. Nicaragua and Togo's were also triangular. By contrast, the shapes of American stamps were boring squares or rectangles.

Eventually, I gave the collection to my son Joel, but the fond memories remain.

Collections for me were more than just physical items. I thought of collections like Mozart forty-one symphonies, and especially Haydn, who composed more than one hundred. I love the Mozart Symphonies after about Number 30, and Haydn's after about 80, and I've collected the music both as recordings and in my memory.

IV. WARWICK STREET

East New York was the name of a kind of ghetto neighborhood in Brooklyn. Actually there were two ghettoes—an Italian one next to the Jewish one. In the earliest days of my youth I thought there were mostly two kinds of people, Italians and Jews, although there was a category called janitors, who were non-Jewish Eastern Europeans. The sign "hot woter" on a rental apartment house reflected a limited command of English, presumably placed there by the janitor.

The parents on our Warwick Street were mostly Jewish immigrants from Eastern Europe, though their offspring were US-born, as I was. Most of them were poor, honest people. That is, all but one large family down the street, who were said to be crooks. We avoided them.

A bit later I discovered that there was another ethnic group, Polish kids who attended parochial school. Still another group I thought of as Americans, wealthy people who owned handsome homes in the area near the Arlington Library and Highland Park. I considered myself Jewish, rather than American, reserved for people with names like Smith, Jones, and White. I had no idea that some were Protestant and others Catholic. They were all gentiles. In school I was taught that we were all Americans. But we were not yet considered equal by others and ourselves.

I was nine years old. We had just moved downscale from an apartment in a middle-class neighborhood to East New York. Grandma, Dad's mother, and her husband owned and lived in a house on Warwick Street. It was during the bowels of the 1933 Depression. We occupied the upstairs flat in their two-story frame house. The walls, both inside and out, were thick with paint layers that covered one another, just as the years covered one another.

And again, another school for me.

PORCH

Transplanted again
to a Brooklyn *shtetl*
to the second floor
of Grandma's small frame house.

Winter mornings rise from the porch
like cream climbing from frozen milk bottles.

Grinding sounds of ashes
and rattling of shoveled coal
remind us, shelter us
from the cold.

Gladiator boys challenge me
to a duel to prove
what I already know
I am too small, too fearful to fight
protected by the sweet-sour warmth
of Grandma's pearl-covered bosom.

PASEY

On our block I was immediately challenged by Pasey, a stocky boy with hair slicked down and a cowlick dangling across his face. Pasey was a few months younger but much heavier and taller than me. I managed to avoid fighting with him, but only with a loss of face. At least I kept my face intact. He confronted me and we had the following conversation.

Pasey pointed his finger in my face.

"What's your name?"

"Albert."

"What kind of sissy name is that?" he said.

"I don't know, what's yours?"

"Pasey," he answered.

I said, "I never heard that name before. What kind is it?"

"Dummy! My Hebrew name is Pesach, so they call me Pasey. My school name is Philip."

"I only have one name," I said.

"Yeah, you pansy, don't you have any other Jewish name your parents call you?"

"No, only Albert. But my grandma calls me Abba. I guess that's Hebrew."

He challenged me. "You want to fight?" He bunched his thick sweater in his fist.

I shrank back, and answered irrelevantly, "I don't know. I'm new here."

Pasey continued, "I can beat you up easy. What class are you in?"

"4A," I said.

He said, "4A1, 2 or 3?" The 1 class was for the faster students.

"I don't know yet. I guess 4A1. I was in 3B1 in the other school."

"Well, I'm only 3B1, but I can still beat you up," Pasey said.

I turned to go. "My grandma called me. I got to go in."

"You sissy! Come on and fight. When you come out I'll get you."

He's bigger than me, much bigger. How can I get away and not look like a sissy? I was so scared, my stomach hurt. I shut it off. I went inside.

"Bubbe, can I have milk and cookies?" I asked.

She gave me a wet kiss on my cheek. I wiped off the stickiness with the back of my hand when she wasn't looking. She spoke only Yiddish. I knew a handful of Yiddish words from listening to Mother and Dad when they spoke Yiddish, as they did at times. I could neither understand most of the language, and of course I couldn't speak Yiddish. But Grandma gave me what I needed and I let her hug and kiss me. I squirmed only a little inside. The trade was worth it—milk, cookies and protection from big Pasey. He was able to talk with Grandma, but I got her love.

Pasey knocked at the door. *"Ich wil Albert sehen."* (I want to see Albert).

"Go away, you bad boy, leave him alone," Grandma said in Yiddish. "He's a good boy."

Gosh! Grandma made it worse. Now when he gets me outside, I got to face being a good boy as well as the new kid.

I looked out the window. It was beginning to get dark. A pushcart peddler went by. Then the Italian ices man. He was singing I-don't-know-what. I guess "Ices." I'd like to get some, but my enemy is outside. Well, I like ice cream much better than ices anyway.

It was getting real dark outside. Mother drew the shades. I was safe inside for the day.

"Go to bed, Albert. It's time," Mother said.

I was worried. New school, new kids, new teachers, and Pasey. If I wish real hard, I might magically make him disappear tonight, so tomorrow I'd be safe.

WARWICK STREET BOYS

I would have to deal with boys who were established there as well as Pasey, They knew their pecking order. As a new kid I had to run the gauntlet. Just as in the barnyard, the roosters deal with a recent arrival. If only my parents had been taller, instead of Mother's four-foot ten and Dad's five-foot two. My inherited short stature made me fair game for my peers and the older guys. I had to be inconspicuous or subservient to avoid fights. I tried not to offend the older boys, but anyway they were too contemptuous to bother me.

Moishe was the clear leader, and chose the games we played. The games were improvised, although tradition played a major part in the choices. At thirteen, Moishe was tough, but not really mean. Vee-chips on the cutting edge of his top two front teeth added to his tough appearance. He acted as a kind of street guard. Once when a gang from a nearby Italian neighborhood invaded our block, Moishe ran them off, a threatening brick in each hand. He didn't have to use the weapons. His show of power was enough. The other boys followed safely behind our leader, and the invaders quickly ran away.

Tied for second in command were Toby and Freddie, Moishe's henchmen.

Quiet-spoken Toby had a pointed mouth with teeth compressed together like the prow of a ship. His jaw was offset to the right and so he talked out of that side of his mouth.

Unlike Toby, Freddie was gabby. He had silky red hair that jumped skyward as he walked. About a year younger than Moishe, Freddie was half-Jewish in this Jewish block, and the only boy other than me who wasn't called by a Jewish nickname. I believe his father, who sat undershirted and unsmiling in a rocker on his wooden porch, was Gentile. Freddie's cousin was Ruth, the only girl close to our age on the block. Tall, round-cheeked with dark blonde hair, she was tomboyish, and only occasionally joined us on the street. Older than the rest of us, she was in the last year of junior high school. She told us about the ditty that boys and girls at the local junior high school sang. "PS 149 is the school for me…" I couldn't remember the rest, but amazingly 75 years after I heard the song, several sites thanks to Google found the rest of the song: "Drives away all adversity. Steady and true we'll be to you. Loyal to 149 RAH RAH!" Danny Kaye went to school there and sang the song according to the same Google search. A computer search tells me that PS 149 is now an elementary school, and named for Danny Kaye. It is located at 700 Sutter Avenue, only nine blocks from our old house on Warwick Street.

Another song Ruth taught us was to the tune of "Songs of the Vagabonds." "Sons of toil and danger, will you serve a stranger and bow down to Burgundy..." The tune was familiar to all. The PS 149 version in part was, "Don't do your homework every night." I couldn't trace the rest of the song that is buried in the annals, not the perennials of my memory.

Moishe gave special recognition to Ruth as a female. He talked about "getting into her pants."

Trying to be one of the guys with my naïve nine-year old mind, I had little idea what he was talking about. I said, "You mean while she's asleep?"

"Of course not, dummy. I want her to know that I'm screwing her." It was just male talk.

The older boys talk about "jerking off."

"What's that?" I asked.

"You play with your prick until you come." said Moshe. Reluctant to show my ignorance I didn't ask, "come where?" But I did ask how to jerk off.

"You just pull on it," Moishe said.

I tried to do it later at home. Nothing happened.

Eventually it did happen. It seemed like a lot of work. But pretty soon, I delighted in the pleasure it gave me to masturbate, as I learned to call it later. I began to have night emissions that were also delicious. I was embarrassed with the hard spots on the sheets when I awoke, that I tried to explain to Mother. In one of her finer moments, she said she understood, and it was natural.

A few years later in my early teens, I enjoyed masturbation so much, I couldn't stop. I felt guilty about my secret pleasure. I put black marks on my calendar and tried to limit how often I masturbated. Though not a scout, I learned from the *Boy Scout's Handbook* that not doing conservation, as they called the act, would prevent one from later marital relations. They avoided the word masturbation, as though reading the M word would cause boys to do it. Sexuality was also an embarrassment for me at times. Rising from a seat on the bus, pun unintended, I often used a book to hide the erection that seemed to haunt me.

It has been said that when boys are asked "Do you masturbate?" Ninety-nine percent say yes, and the other one percent is lying.

The song "Shanghai Lil," appeared in a 1933 movie, *Footlight Parade*. Moishe made gestures with his hands while singing the words to the song, "I've been looking high (breasts) and I've been looking low (vagina), looking for my Shanghai Lil." There were also jokes about Mae West, the sexy blonde of the era.

One of the boys found a book, the name of which escapes me. The title might have been White Tower (not the mountain book), or White Castle (certainly not the hamburger place), or something like that. There was a sexy passage in the book, and we all peered greedily at the page over Moishe's shoulder.

Private homes often had finished basements, and some had social clubs that met there. Once we saw a woman running away from a basement. A man ran after her, while buttoning his fly. "They must be white slavers," Moishe, said. He had heard about white slavery from newspapers.

The chaser probably was up to no good, although I doubt that it involved white slavery.

However, it made for a more sensational tale.

AN ALMOST SCARY ADVENTURE

The boys nicknamed Hawkeye for his almost-closed eyelids that made him appear to be barely awake. He was my age and both were on the bottom of the Warwick Street totem pole, generally ignored by the older, bigger, tougher boys and last to be picked for choose-up teams. So we often came together to make our own plans. Hawkeye and I talked about visiting the graveyard in Highland Park at night, a Tom Sawyer kind of adventure. We planned to meet at midnight, after we were supposed to be in bed, tiptoe out, and sneak off to the isle of the dead, a mile away. It was a great idea, one full of excitement and pretty scary. That made it all the more exciting. I wish I could say what a wonderful adventure it was. Unfortunately, it never happened. Neither of us was willing to confront an escape from parental safety and possible ghosts in the graveyard.

A few blocks away, past Blake Avenue, past Dumont Avenue, almost to New Lots Avenue, was the Italian neighborhood. There was some rivalry, although little hostility between the Italian boys and us. But boys are boys and eruptions could take place. I enjoyed walking through their neighborhood when I felt my intrusion was safe. Their small backyards were like minuscule farms, invariably with grapevines, to be made into wine. I loved inhaling the inviting fragrance of fermenting grapes. A yeasty scent perfumed the air on fall days.

Fermenting yeast from wine still excites my nasal memory. Remembering the aroma of yeast from the bakery on Warwick Street intensifies the memory.

People stood in line at Wisotsky's corner bakery when fresh Kaiser rolls emerged from the oven, their warm fragrance enveloping the street. Mother had the notion that those soft breads were indigestible. And so my family always missed those tempting fresh rolls and ate the day-old ones, barely edible, and unexciting to my taste buds.

BOYS AND THEIR GAMES

> Ailey-Bailey, a bundle of straw
> Belching is against the law
> Hit me now, hit me then
> Hit me when I belch again.

Boys chanted this ditty on our street. Sometimes they substituted the word *grepse*, the Yiddish word for belch. When a boy *grepsed* the other boys punched him in the upper arms until he recited five brands of cigarettes. At times they changed it to five makes of cars. The procedure was the same if one farted, only the hits were harder and one had to recite seven brands, as a hierarchy of offensiveness.

Oops, I belched! "Camels, Chesterfields, Old Gold, Philip Morris, Luckies." What a relief! I received only ten hits, and my arms hurt only slightly. Uh-oh, a loud fart escaped. I couldn't think of other brands. Meanwhile, they pounded away and my arms were smarting. Oh yes, "Kools and Menthols."

"Menthols ain't a brand!" the boys yelled, and the pounding continued. The rules didn't allow running away.

"Oh yeah, Pall Mall," I said.

My arms ached. This was not a good time to play knucks. All our games were competitive, and most were physical, including this card game. Starting with five cards each, the loser was the one left with cards in his hand, like the game of Old Maid. The deck was squared, the loser made a fist, and each of the other players took turns hitting him on top of his knuckles with the deck, according to the number of cards he was left with. If any of the winners dropped the deck, it was fifty-two-pickup and the other players including the loser got to hit the dropper fifty-two strokes. I was very careful to hold the deck firmly when I was on the winning side.

A crueler version of the game allowed the torturers to arrange the cards with their edges on a slant. That could really tear up skin. Fortunately, kinder souls, (did they exist?) or more likely a leader who once suffered severely in our neighborhood decided to outlaw slanting the deck.

This time I was left with ten cards. With five other players, I was in for fifty raps. As the torture progressed, my hand went from white to pink to scarlet. I didn't dare express pain out loud, but my inner voice went from ow to ooh to oy! It was tough being the newest and the smallest, wishing for the acceptance that I never got.

I lurched homeward, my sore arms dangling gorilla-like, my knuckles like glowing coals.

Another game was Johnny on the Pony.

The leader of one team was Moishe. The opposing leader was Toby or Freddie. Each leader held up a fist and chose even or odd. Simultaneously they snapped up either one finger or two, that determined which team had first choice.

One boy was the pillow. He stood up. The others on the defense team were ponies and bent over. The first in line tucked his head between the pillow's legs and wrapped his arms around them. Pillows were typically lightweight or weaker guys. Each of the others tucked his head between the legs of the boy ahead and wrapped his arms similarly. And so there was a chain of heads down, backs horizontal. One at a time each member of the aggressor team placed his hands on the end boy and using him as a springboard, leapt as hard as he could on the backs of the other team. The objective was to collapse a pony. The strategy was to pile as many boys on a single victim, preferably a weak one, forcing him to collapse. When all the second team had jumped, the leader called out, "Johnny on the pony, Johnny on the pony, Johnny on the pony, one, two, three." All got off, and the episode was over. If any link collapsed during this time, the teams repeated the game. Sometimes a pony collapsed even before all the team members had their turn. If the defense was able to resist falling, the teams changed places and the losers had a chance to get even.

One of these times Hawkeye was the pillow, and I was at the opposite end. The jumpers concentrated on me. Toby sprang on my back, close to my shoulders. Pasey was next. His big, navy woven sweater made him seem even heavier than he was. I'd never seen him without that woolen sweater. I suspected he must have even worn it to bed. He jumped on my butt, riding back-saddle behind Toby. I collapsed. I didn't know which was worse, my back that felt broken or the abuse from my teammates for literally letting them down. My limp got no sympathy after I picked myself up from the ground.

I went home, scrunched down like the Hunchback of Notre Dame.

Sometimes I wonder—how did I, how did we, survive childhood?

Not all games were equally rough. We had so-called seasons. Not winter spring, summer, or fall, but game seasons, with no obvious relationship to the position of the sun, but which mysteriously appeared one day and disappeared as silently. It was as though a magic spell was cast, and suddenly yo-yos were the rage. Within a day, we all hauled out our yo-yos and were outdoors spinning them.

There was also a season for tops. The narrow end of some tops was pointed; others had a ball bearing-like end. We wrapped a sturdy cord tightly around the pear-shaped wooden toy. A loop at one end of a strong cord stayed on our finger as we spun the top toward the pavement. The competition was to see whose top could spin the longest. A boy hurled his top on that of a competitor, to stop it from spinning. If he threw a pointed one with enough force, he might even split his adversary's top.

Other games were played at any time of year. All we needed was a hollow rubber ball, a Spaldeen, Brooklynese for the trade name Spalding.

Box-ball required a large chalked square facing another opposite it. You bounced the ball from your box to the opponents, who tried to return it by hitting it back into your box.

Handball was played against any suitable wall, often the brick side of an apartment house. In standard handball one hit the wall directly. After a bounce, the opponent returned the ball. An alternative was Chinese handball, in which you hit the ball so it bounced once before it contacted the wall and similarly returned.

Stickball was (and I assume still is) a classic city substitute for baseball, using a broomstick as bat and a Spaldeen as the ball. It was played in the street. Hitting prowess was measured in sewers, the distance between metal lids that cover the opening to sewers in the middle of the street. A two-sewer hit, at least 200 feet, was virtually a home run.

Typically at my turn at bat, I swung at the ball, but I never achieved a two-sewer hit; in fact I often struck out. If I did hit the ball, most often it sadly trickled down from my stick. I was consigned to the outfield, way out where few balls ever reached, and I rarely caught even those distant ones.

Punchball was played like stickball, but the person up used his fist instead of a stick. Boys on the opposing team fielded the Spaldeen and tried to touch the runner out. What would we have done without those noble rubber spheres from Davega's sports store?

In the game of Ringelevio. team members were pursued and captured by being grabbed, often by their sweaters. They were then hauled off to a den guarded by a member of the competitor team. Prisoners could be freed by one of their teammates invading the den, at the risk of being captured in the process. Mothers complained about sweaters torn or stretched beyond recall from this game.

These and many other games passed from one generation to another, a tribute to the ingenuity of kids who found inexpensive ways to have fun.

A favorite solo pastime was to stick a well-chewed piece of gum to the end of a broomstick and fish for dropped coins through grill-work that covered the cellar opening of bakeries. We rarely got rich this way, but it was a challenge, and the scent of yeast vented from bakeries was a heady side effect.

We learned to make many sounds with our mouths. Younger boys made sounds of cars, planes, and motorcycles. As we got older we made farting sounds. Sometimes when a guy mouthed a loud farting sound, his friend would say, "Now do it with your mouth," implying that it had been a real fart. Other fart sounds were made by placing the left hand under the right armpit and swinging the right arm toward the body. This was even more effective if the armpit was moist, as on sticky summer days.

So-called raspberries were made by vibrating the lips or the tongue. They were often targeted at competitors in baseball stadiums.

Boys had their own expressions. If someone was blocking

your view, you might say, "Is your father a glazier?" If you felt too hurried by a boy, "What's the rush? You weren't born in a hurry." If a boy blocked a player in a handball game, it was a "hindu," or hindrance.

Of course girls had their own culture. They walked arm in arm and sang pop songs, using the latest lyrics from "cheat sheets," printed weekly in the thirties and forties. Some of their games were jacks, and skipping rope, accompanied by doggerel verse, or counting, "5-10-15-20..."

SEASONS

SUMMER DAY ESCAPE

Nine year olds sent out to play
on August city streets
we find respite in the cool netherworld—
basement of an apartment house
where we devour pulpy literature
    Detective Fiction Weekly
    Dime Detective
    Argosy
their dank sweet-sour scent
heightens the stories we feast upon

When the streets swallow the sun
we stash our print-food
our hunger assuaged
for another summerday banquet.

AUTUMN

How delightful to hear the crunch of dry maple leaves as my steps smashed them. I crunch, crunch, crunched my way, and enjoyed the drum beat of my walking. But the *piece de resistance* of fall was the perfumed air, the acrid, intoxicating scent of smoldering leaves that householders piled and burned at the curb. Autumn, the seducer, knew that cold would soon surround us.

WINTER

On a winter's late afternoon I wandered past the Italian neighborhood toward New Lots Avenue. The season had been heavy with snow. The city had cleared snow from the streets and piled it up on sidewalk corners. I climbed the tallest of the piles and played king of the lumpy hill. My kingdom was white and tinged with the gray soot of the streets and furnaces. It was my Everest. I climbed my mountain, jumped down, boots stomping, and climbed again, blood racing through my veins. I was thrilled with the imaginary adventure, aware that darkness was overtaking me. I didn't want to face mother's berating, but I made one last ascension of my peak. Well, maybe another one for the road, as I heard adults say. At last, reluctantly, I headed back toward Sutter Avenue and home.

Other winter pleasures were snowball fights. My freezing paws fashioned snowballs and threw them against any attractive targets— lampposts, ash cans, or girls walking by. If there was no more prey, I tossed them up high and shouted, " Boom!" as they splatted on the ground, like grenades.

A special treat on cold days was the Italian vendor in his wagon, with steam whistling and wafting the chestnut fragrance into the winter air.

SPRING

After too long a season of cold, followed by a rainy April, a burst of spring took me by surprise. One morning I looked out through the raindrops on my window. Grasses had shot up suddenly like Jack in the Beanstalk. Where did those yellow, blue, and orange flowers magically suddenly come from? Outdoors, the air was scented with the perfume of those dazzling flowers.

It is different in California, where I live. Here, wet winter slides into spring, unlike the sharper seasonal changes of the Northeast, my native land.

PUBLIC LIBRARY

I loved the local Arlington Library. I don't recall whether the neighborhood boys went there. We never talked about it. The uncomfortable part of the mile walk was when I had to pass a Catholic school, where boys played in the yard. If I stopped for a moment to see the game, they shouted, "Get outta here, you dirty Jew." Fortunately, the yard was fenced, so they reached me only with their voices. After the first few times, I rushed past the school to avoid their hostility. How did they know I was Jewish? By my face, my scent? I wasn't wearing a Star of David, nor a yarmulke. Years later referring to her experience in stores Mother said, "Oh, *they* know." But I think that was left over from her childhood experiences in Russia.

On Saturdays the librarians read stories to us. I learned about Thor and the other Norse gods before I knew of the Greek and Roman gods. Loki was my favorite for his trickster ways.

The library offered many adventure books that I enjoyed reading. Also I checked out books on wood construction, authored mostly by Archie Frederick Collins. I never built things of wood, since I had neither tools nor wood. It was an unfulfilled dream, but I kept reading the books and dreaming. Years later as an adult, I had my own workshop and made things out of wood—bookcases, shelves, and the like. But the boyhood fantasies were more varied than practical.

Recently I heard about a new book, *The Dangerous Book For Boys*, by Conn and Hal Iggullden, I was surprised and delighted that my local library owned a copy. I turned the pages and my eyes misted. What I read reminded me of my boyhood. I yearn for those years, and some of the childhood joys I had, as well as those I missed having. Oh, to be a boy of ten again! Of course I had to have my own copy of the book. Sometimes I peruse that magical book and close my eyes and dream of the past.

THE TELEPHONE

Only a small minority of families could afford to own a telephone. However, there was a coin telephone in Meyerowitz's candy store on the corner. We boys hung around the store, and when the phone rang, we would race to take the call, often for a phone-less resident in the neighborhood. The messenger ran to announce the call, hoping to earn a tip, perhaps a cent or two, occasionally a nickel, and rarely a dime. If one received a quarter— an extraordinary event—the lucky boy felt truly wealthy!

One day I had three library books that were due. Instead of returning the books, I chose to hang around the phone instead. After several hours during which I succeeded in answering the phone twice, I collected four cents in tips. Since overdue fines were two cents a day for each book, I was two cents in the hole for the books. Another reason for delaying the return, was that I felt uncomfortable passing the parochial school where the kids insulted me. Of course I had to pay the piper the next day on both counts.

I finally got the message: I had better pay what I owe before trying to get rich. I wish I had heeded the other message, "Stop stalling," a lesson that I often ignore.

HIGHLAND PARK

Highland Park straddles the border between Brooklyn and Queens. The park was a mile from my house, across Sutter Avenue, past Pitkin Avenue, under the Elevated at Fulton Street, and past the Arlington Avenue library; I could walk there from our house. I enjoyed strolling around the reservoir and looking at the gravestones in nearby Cypress Hills National Cemetery.

One day near the reservoir I found a pamphlet full of words that condemned Jews as bad people and Christ-killers. I was upset. I tore the pamphlet into shreds and pissed on it.

Many years later a Catholic girl friend told me she thought the pamphlet was part of the ultraconservative Baltimore catechism.

Mentioning pissing reminds me of the word pishy, that my mother used, particularly when I was very young. Another word for urinating was "doing your duty." Sometimes peeing was called "number one," as opposed to "number two," defecating. The other word for the latter was "eh-eh." Such were some euphemisms in my time.

YMCA

One weekend I learned of a coupon for one free entry to the swimming pool at the local YMCA. I cut the coupon out from the sepia-colored rotogravure section of the *New York Daily Mirror*. I loved swimming, but there were no public pools nearby, and so I readily accepted the pass. A requirement was that we had to swim naked, and so I stripped before entering the pool. I felt very conspicuous, the only circumcised boy there, the only one without a penis end-cap. It was as though I were wearing a Star of David. I was embarrassed and tried to cross my legs to hide my difference. Less than five years later the mark of David became a way the Nazis could check to know which boys and men were Jewish. So much for "passing," although there was no indication that the free swim was limited to Christian boys. Ironically, after college I had a room at the Greenwich, Connecticut YMCA and was elected Mayor of the residents. During the campaign my poster read, "Don't be a sloth, man, vote for Roth-man!"

Grandma Sophie, Mother, Dad, and me, 1927

BUBBE AND ZEYDE

Bubbe (Grandma) Sophie was Dad's mother, my only surviving grandparent. *Bubbe* spoke almost no English. Her language was Yiddish, the language of the *shtetl* in Eastern Europe. I knew little Yiddish. So she communicated with me with hugs. She doted on us, her two grandchildren. I have a photograph of Grandma looking down with a loving smile at my baby brother. She sometimes called him humorously, but fondly, a *shaygets* or gentile male, since he was so blond. I understood the Yiddish when her words crooned, "*Abbela, Ich lebe ovf dir*, or Dear Albert, I love you. She was Old World, born in Bessarabia, a part of Russia-Rumania. She migrated to the US in 1918 along with my father and her husband Max. She had married Max after the death of my dad's father, who had died before I was born. *Abbela* is the diminutive of Abba, the Hebrew name I was given in honor of my dead grandfather, as was customary in Jewish tradition. My name Albert is an English rendition of the Hebrew.

Grandmother was a bosomy short presence, tight as a mummy in a corseted dress. Her scent was stale, but not unpleasant, a *Bubbe* smell. Her gray hair looked like curly metal wires pulled into a bun. A simple set of pearls draped her neck. When she smiled, teeth glittered gold in her mouth. Her furniture also was simple. The dark brown bureau with its curved front was covered with a doily that draped over the sides. A few hairpins were scattered on the doily.

Unlike his mother, my father wasn't orthodox, perhaps not even a believer. I don't recall that he was ever explicit about his religious beliefs or lack of them. An obedient son, he went along with her orthodoxy, and Mother kept a kosher kitchen while we lived in her house. Dad went to Temple more or less weekly, and certainly on holy days.

Grandma's house was heated by a coal-fired furnace in

the cellar. I can still imagine the scraping sound of coal being shoveled, and the smell of ashes removed from the stove as a wave of dust filled my nostrils.

Bubbe had an extensive vegetable garden in the long backyard. She also had an esthetic side. Flowers were a part of her garden. Blue and white irises with their familiar scent still remind me of her.

Shade from an adjacent apartment house kept part of the yard constantly damp. Bricks on the wall of the nearby house, and even the wooden posts of the grape arbor were partly covered with moss. I still associate moss growing on bricks and pavements with Grandma's yard.

The cellar was a scary place. A pair of slanted wooden doors in the yard opened outward. Steps led down to a vertical door to the basement. I felt uncomfortable entering that dark, dank cellar, with creeping bugs and spider webs that brushed my face. That very fear was like a magnet, attracting me to the place.

Grandpa kept his house painting supplies in a locked shack at the back of the yard. Grandpa, *Zeyde* in Yiddish, was tall and lean, with gray stubble on his face. His cheeks appeared sunken, topped by his high cheekbones. His face was sprinkled with dried droplets of white paint. I never saw him without a gray Fedora covering his head. Orthodox Jews always have their heads covered. He was frequently unshaven, especially on *Shabbes*, the Saturday Sabbath, when shaving was forbidden. Also proscribed were lighting a fire, switching on a light, or using scissors. To keep the day holy, he hired a boy to light the kitchen stove on Saturday, The boy was known as *a Shabbes goy*, meaning a gentile, free from the Jewish proscriptions. On another day the boy received payment for his service, since handling money was also unholy on the Sabbath.

Grandpa used few words that often sounded like growls in

his Yiddish. I might greet him with, "Hello, Zeyde." His response was a grumpy "Mm." He was aloof, indifferent toward me, but not unkind. I thought it was just his way. Only later I learned that he wasn't my blood relative. He had married Grandma after my real grandfather died, long before I was born. I had always thought of his grandchildren as my cousins. When he saw Fayge and his other his grandchildren, Zeyde's manner was transformed. His face beaming, he said with warmth, *"Mein libene kinder,"* My dear children.

ZEYDE, BUBBE

Always a gray Fedora
covenant head cover
gray stubble on leather face
gaunt cheeks creased
    like hillcountry folds
his face clown-like, sprayed
with spots of house paint
paint that provides his Depression pittance.
Husband to widowed Sophie
my Bubbe, my grandma
he ignores me grumpily
not my Zeyde, my real grandfather.
    Bubeh knows only Yiddish
    I don't understand
She speaks to me with hugs and cheek kisses
    I do understand.
It is more than enough.

CAT ATTACK!

One morning I awoke while my parents were still asleep. I walked into our bathroom. When Grandma's gray cat perched on a cabinet saw me, the crouching tiger leapt. I screamed, thinking I was about to be attacked. Mother and Dad came running, and Grandma climbed the stairs from below. Probably the cat was trying to avoid being cornered, and jumped past me. But Grandma's little boy was precious to her, and so the cat was banished from the household. Poverty made for practical people. The cat had been kept as a mouser, rather than as a pet. The mice must have had a field day until a substitute filled the feline void.

PUBLIC SCHOOL 158

Often when I transferred to a new school I was placed in the slow class. In a few days I would be sent to the fast class, where I belonged. In the third grade in PS 158, I quickly rose to the top of the fast class, except for Malcolm. In previous years, I had always been at the top. But I couldn't beat Malcolm, a slight boy with wavy dark hair. His nose seemed constantly blocked, and he snorted, trying to clear the passages.

In arithmetic class our teacher gave us so-called Factor cards. These had multiplication and division exercises printed on them. We were supposed to solve the problems and check with the teacher when finished. If all the problems were correct, we were given a new Factor card. In retrospect that was a helluva way to teach and learn—merely repeating the process *ad nauseam*. In retrospect it seems strange that we were not given more challenging material.

I could never beat Malcolm's speed. After that class, I remained number one throughout my years in elementary school. I was more competitive than I realized, since I never liked losing to Malcolm. Later in a different school, a teacher called out our IQ scores. I feel that was inappropriate. I was the top student, but Lenny Bernstein (no, not that one!) had a few IQ points higher than mine. I resented his bragging about it. In my mind I was supposed to be the top student in every respect, another reflection of my competitiveness.

MY BODYGUARD

In 1933 when I entered PS 158, the fifth school in my educational journey, some boys picked on me as usual. One of them, about my size, kept pushing and poking me. In previous encounters I would have just walked away. This time, however, I stood there and warned him, but he persisted. He poked me once more. I blew up and pummeled him mercilessly, my head facing down like a charging bull. I bloodied his nose, and from then on he avoided me as if I were a cactus.

Other bigger guys still tried to pick on me. Then along came Angelo. He was tall, he was strong, he was determined. Somehow he took a liking to me. The word got out that anybody who bothered Albert would have to deal with Angelo. From then on, I was off-limits to the bullies and I could wander in the schoolyard with impunity, backed by my dependable bodyguard. Angelo was very different from me. I a Jewish kid, a gifted student, and he an Italian-American, in a slower class in school. We had met in the schoolyard, and somehow we clicked. He had a big toothy grin that belied his toughness that could be called into action. Together we were just like the plot in the 1980 movie, *My Bodyguard*. I fancy that they stole the idea from me!

When I changed schools and lost Angelo, I had to depend on my own power. Once again I became a victim, thanks to my small size and my peaceful demeanor, or perhaps my cowardice.

TEACHERS

Mrs. Watt was not a woman you would pick out in a crowd. She was homely in the old-fashioned sense of the word, that is, plain looking, like a woman from home—perhaps a favorite aunt. Her dark, kinky hair tinged with gray strands was tied in an unkempt bun. Short hairs grew out of a mole on her chin. She had a matronly bosom. I don't recall that she ever raised her voice, yet she usually had the class's attention.

Most of the teachers in the seven elementary schools I attended remain a blur in memory, but over seventy years later I remember her clearly, though I was in her class for only half a year.

We did spatter prints of leaves and learned to recognize trees—gingko, Norway maple, oaks and others that grew in Brooklyn. She expressed love for things that grew and stirred in me an awareness of nature's treasures. She also seemed to care deeply about her students.

On her own time one Saturday Mrs. Watt brought our class to Prospect Park, the largest park in Brooklyn. We identified trees and visited the zoo. Her husband, a tall, erect man accompanied us as well. "Here, children, I've got ice cream for all of you," he said. What a treat for us kids in that Depression year of 1933!

I don't remember details of the zoo visit, except the sweet creaminess of the vanilla cone on my tongue and ice cream's slow disappearance down my throat.

I feel a warm glow as I think fondly about Mrs. Watt. My strong connection to trees, wildflowers and love of hiking may have sprouted from the seeds she helped implant in me.

MRS. JOHNSON AND MUSIC APPRECIATION

Music appreciation was required in the New York City public schools at the time. What a pity that music appreciation is no longer in the curriculum in many if not most schools!

Mrs. Johnson was another teacher I remember well. I can hear her sing, "This is a song in B, that Schubert wrote but never finished." Mrs. Johnson's quavering soprano gave words to a movement in Schubert's Eighth Symphony in B-minor, his Unfinished Symphony. Later we would be tested on it. She hummed various tunes, and we were expected to know the title and composer of the work. We sang phrases such as, "Moment Musicale, written by Schubert," and "To a Wild Rose from MacDowell's Woodland Sketches, like a wild rose its melody fair." Those were the words of musical educators, not the composers. Singing the words was supposed to help us to remember the music. For me it was effective. I still can recall those words and music. On the other hand, years later those words at times intruded on my enjoyment of the music. But time has mellowed me somewhat, and I appreciate that we had been exposed to classical music as part of our education.

Returning to sweet, coffee-colored Mrs. Johnson. She sang the words, "At Dawn from William Tell's Overture by Rossini," to the tune of the music. But she evidently didn't feel the tunefulness of the movement known as "The Storm." Instead, she made a jumble of noise to imitate the storm. I told my former nemesis Pasey, that there was a tune to this movement, and hummed it for him. He was amazed, and told the other boys on the street about my remarkable (!) prowess. Perhaps I made a few points with them that partly compensated for my lack of athletic ability.

MORE MUSIC

"Music hath charms to soothe the savage breast." My early education biased me toward musicality and classical music in particular. Even the popular song writers of the thirties, forties, and some since then have musical quality, and the words show intelligence and sensitivity. The Gershwins, Cole Porter, Rodgers and Hart and others had brilliant lyrics and lovely melodies. I find that some music today, young female singers that scream or shout the words to current songs don't seem musical to my ear. I guess I have not kept up with changing times.

OTHER TEACHERS

There were less gentle teachers. "Slaughter House Slattery" was one teacher's self-described title. With her Irish bulldog face, she was tough, but a good and fair-minded teacher, her bark much stronger than her bite. I liked her and I thought she liked me.

A tall, almost masculine, no-nonsense gym teacher, Mrs. Herzog was in charge of our school assemblies. I wondered why she chose to give the honor of carrying the flag always to the same athletic boy. The procession of the flag accompanied a Sousa military march, played on a piano.

WHERE IS THY STING?

Death was a strange, shocking new experience for me, as I suppose it was for other children in the class.

Little Norman was a slight, blue eyed, blond boy in our class. Quiet and unassuming, he made only a slight impression on us. He missed school for a week. We were told that Norman had the dreaded pneumonia, indeed, the horrible double pneumonia. A few weeks later, Norman appeared in class. We all breathed more easily. A day later, he was absent again. After another week, the teacher told us that Norman had died of pneumonia. I didn't know what to think. How could this be? A nine-year old boy shouldn't die, should he? Could this happen to me? Where was Norman now?

RADISHES

A happier memory was that of Marvin, a dark-haired boy with slightly slanted eyes and puffy, almost girlish white cheeks. After school on his way to Hebrew studies, he munched on radishes that he ate like candy. He always had a plentiful supply, and offered some to me. Now when I bite into one, I think of Marvin's radish joy. Did he continue to enjoy his red edibles as an adult?

NITS

Florence, a freckled blonde girl was kept out of school in the fourth grade in PS 158. She had tiny gold earrings, more typically worn by Italian girls, and unusual for Jewish girls at the time. We heard that she had nits. "Nits? What are they," we asked.

Our teacher, Mrs. Johnson, carefully told us that they are the eggs of lice.

"Can we catch them from her?" Mrs. Johnson was on the spot.

Well," she said, "Lice can easily move from head to head, and so Florence probably got them from another person."

We looked at one another suspiciously, alarmed and disgusted by the thought. We decided they were cooties, which we had heard of on the street.

Did the teacher make a serious ethical breach? How else could she answer our question? She was tactful in describing this repulsive subject. In those days some teachers were openly or surreptitiously insulting, and by contrast, Mrs. Johnson was certainly kind.

Of course, we all kept our distance from poor Florence, for fear of catching her cooties.

CHAPTER V. WARWICK STREET, PART 2

KOCHALEIN IN THE CATSKILLS

It was the terrible thirties. We often look at the past with rose-colored nostalgia. But during the years of the Great Depression many instances of individual depression were a consequence of the big one. My father was only intermittently employed during most of the thirties. Anxious about where the food and rent money would come from, he often looked worried. But he took care of us, at times in quasi-legal activities, by selling on the streets without the costly permit required by New York City. He sold whatever he could— all I remember were women's summer hats and condoms. He had a supply of the latter that I found in his chifforobe, an old term for a kind of bureau. Optimistically I helped myself to a few condoms but they remain unused.

During this era, the man of the family was expected to be the lone provider. Of course, Mother also had to make do and keep up the family spirits. We had sufficient and healthful foods— chicken, steak, and vegetables, and even whole grains, thanks to Mother's choices. Dad somehow found the wherewithal to send Mother, my brother, and me to the country for two successive summers near the peak of the Depression.

There were some elegant resort hotels In the Catskills, often humorously referred to as the Yiddish Alps and the Borscht Belt. They had fancy meals, swimming pools, and social directors who organized activities, including the evening entertainment. Many performers of the past and even more recent comedians and singers originally began their careers as entertainers in those hotels—Red Buttons and Eddie Fisher, among others. We certainly could not afford those hotels and stayed instead at a rooming house called a *Kochalein*, or cook alone, translated from the Yiddish. In typical Jewish sardonic humor, *Kochalein* was translated facetiously as cook yourself, sort of auto-cannibalism. These rooming houses probably had been hotels during prosperous times before the Depression. They kept their previous names, though any semblance of elegance was gone.

The man of the family "bached" it during the week. On some weekends he rode up in a shared limousine to spend a few days with his family. The limousines were not the ones that today bring one in relative comfort to the airport nor the elegant ones that carry teens on prom night. They were converted from oversized taxis or undersized buses. They carried about sixteen or eighteen people. When our family first went to the country, I remember riding in one of those limos and staring out the window at trees and mountains seemingly without end, an unusual sight for a city boy.

The first summer we stayed at a place in Mountaindale, New York. Each family had a room upstairs with several beds. In the community kitchen below, each woman had one of a bank of gas rings available for cooking her family's meals. The wives competed for precious space on storage shelves and in the group refrigerators. I was too young to pay attention to such adult details. I can only imagine the squabbles that women must have had about shared spaces and who purloined whose food.

My memory of the place consists of flypapers, curly brown, twisting in breeze from the overhead fan. Cemented by their still buzzing wings, flies vainly tried to escape.

I have few clear memories of that summer, except that my younger brother Eddy was scalded when he passed too close to a woman carrying a pot of boiling water. He wasn't seriously hurt, but everyone's attention turned to him, and once more I felt ignored.

The second summer, we stayed at the Kiamesha Villa, a rather pretentious title for a less-than-modest place, in the village of Kiamesha, A year older, I was allowed to run about with less parental oversight.

Recently I turned on the radio to hear Lena Horne singing "Stormy Weather." I became that ten year old in my imagination, riding in a limo with my parents and other passengers to the resort in the Catskills. A car radio was playing "Stormy Weather," and it was raining. We stopped at a gasoline station to fill up. I got a free comic book there that served as an advertisement for Gulf gasoline. I was eating a sandwich of chopped sour pickle immersed in cream cheese. Even now I salivate at the thought of that sandwich. I'd like to have a clone of it, if I could only find a real kosher sour pickle where I live, but California isn't New York.

Those modest rooming houses had no swimming pools, bands, or famous entertainers. We did have a sort of social director, who organized games, dances, and told jokes. Perhaps he was paid, or received a discount from the modest cost for a stay at the place. Maybe he simply liked to act out an unfulfilled desire to don a microphone. He also conducted a Friday night Jewish service, the only one that I recall ever having attended. I suspect my mother wanted to keep me away from Jewish lore and religious observances, as part of being assimilated into the mainstream American culture. I did learn a few Hebrew holy songs such as "*Ainkelo hainu*" at the Kiamesha Villa.

Entertainment was a makeshift affair. I took part with other children in a skit for the amusement of the adults who enjoyed Yiddish. The setting was a fantasy poker game. Each of the players took turns betting. The first bet was one Milk of Magnesia. Another followed with two Feenamints, and a third, three ExLax, all heavily advertised products to relieve constipation. When it was time to call the bets, there were a pair of aces, two pairs of kings, and three of a kind. I groaned, "*Oy, ich hob* (I have) *a fuller hoisen*, that is, a full house. The adults roared with laughter. *Hoizen* is also the word for pants.

Those summers gave me a chance to see grasslands and woods. I discovered the fun that country boys knew, picking huckleberries from wild bushes, and walking in warm cowpies. Although we lacked a swimming pool, a fellow conspirator and I learned when a nearby luxury hotel had its dinner hour. We climbed over the locked fence and jumped into the pool. Mother scolded me when she saw my telltale wet hair. I wasn't permitted a second pool escapade.

We kids built a fire to roast marshmallows when our parents were out of reach. A boy suddenly rushed off to pee. In a hurry to return to the fire, he neglected to put his penis back into his pants. His cousin observed this and alerted all of us to the "free show," as we used to call it. When he realized what had happened, he angrily ran after her. I remember thinking at the time that I would have died if this had happened to me. But he lived through it, and our activities continued.

I was attracted to Sydelle. We had an innocent romance. At the end of the summer, our relationship ended, since I lived in Brooklyn and she in The Bronx, more than an hour apart by subway.

The days of *Kochalein* are gone, although recent immigrant groups may have resurrected the institution of rooming houses in the Catskills. My experience of the outdoors during that time gave this city-bred boy another taste of the joys of nature that fed my appetite for woods and open country. Later in my adulthood I became an avid hiker and nature-lover.

MOVIES

The first movie I remember was at an outdoor theater in summer, close to the elevated train structure on Pitkin Avenue. Three or four years old, I sat next to my mother and father. I have no memory of the film.

In a movie I saw later, gorilla hands reached from behind a woman to strangle her in her bed. The recollection was faint, but such memories are like old shirts that have faded. They're still there, but they are barely usable.

THE GALLOPING GHOST

Movies played an important part of my life. Saturday was movie day at the Loew's Warwick or the Pitkin. Five cents in 1934 entitled us to a double feature that often included a romantic musical with handsome Dick Powell. His films were variously about the Navy, West Point, and Broadway, before his later dramatic detective roles. The words to a song from one of his romantic films pop into my mind, "Shipmates stand forever, don't give up the ship." Though the locales varied, the story and songs were similar, and the female lead often was Ruby Keeler. The musical love stories affected the way I saw relationships in my childhood. I became a secret romantic. Unconsciously I wanted a model of what the movies showed, a completely unreal portrayal of what a relationship was and ought to be between the sexes.

The *piece de resistance* was the serial, presented weekly in ten or twelve parts, each ending with suspense. I *had* to see next week's installment.

One serial was "The Galloping Ghost," the designated name given to Red Grange, a football hero from Notre Dame. I can't remember the stories, but the name Galloping Ghost stirred my imagination.

There were plenty of Western movies. My favorite cowboy was Tom Mix, who was in many movies with his horse Tony. He seemed to be the embodiment of what a cowboy should be—a fast rider, and a tough, lantern-jawed, quiet-spoken man.

RADIO PROGRAMS

On his radio show Uncle Don told kids to have manners and behave. He had fictional characters like Willapus Wallapus and Susan Bedusan, to exemplify his lessons. A legend was that one day after signing off, he remarked, "That should take care of the little bastards for now," unaware that the microphone was still on. Poor Uncle Don! That ended his career, whether or not it was the truth.

A humorous program featured two bumbling detectives, Black and Blue. One of their tongue-in-cheek mottoes was, "We always get our man." Another comic, Joe Penner, had throaty lines like "Hyuk, hyuk, hyuk." Often he feigned crying. But his craziest lines were, "You *nasty* man," and "Wanna buy a duck?" His popularity was short-lived, as was his life. He died not long after his radio program had run a year.

Other radio programs I listened to were Little Orphan Annie and Jack Armstrong, the All-American Boy, who may be better remembered for his sponsor, Wheaties.

I wonder whether I am one of the few people in America who remembers these forgotten programs— Red Davis, a teenager in Pepper Young's Family and The Bobby Benson Adventures on the H-Bar-O Ranch, sponsored appropriately by H-O Cooking Oats.

In my early teens, "Mama, Oh Mama, that man's here again! Ohhh yeah!" were the introductory words to Al Pierce's weekly show. Even Mother enjoyed the program, and she always laughed at those first words.

The Aldrich Family, a popular radio situation comedy was remembered for its introduction—his mother calling, "Hen-reeeee! Hen-ree Al-drich!" The awkward teen Henry Aldrich responded loudly, "Coming, Mother, coming!" in his adolescent high-pitched voice that cracked. Ezra Stone was the actor that originally portrayed him.

Kaltenmeyer's Kindergarten radio program was loaded with stereotypes. Among others were kids with German and Scandinavian accents, but the ones that stood out in my mind were a woman with an exaggerated Italian accent, and a boy with a Yiddish accent who constantly said, "Isidore is-a-doorman." The program at the time seemed hilarious. By current standards it would be considered politically incorrect.

CARTOONS

I enjoyed cartoons in the daily papers and comic books. Unabashedly I admit that as an adult I continue to read the comics in the newspapers.

The original Big Little Books, were square pulpy volumes about four inches square and a few inches thick, with stiff covers. On each page was a captioned cartoon opposite the text on the facing page. I used to own the first one published by the Whitman Company, *The Adventures of Dick Tracy.* Though only ten cents in 1932 when the cartoon book emerged, it has become a sought-after memento that sells for hundreds or even a thousand dollars.

Even earlier a single-frame cartoon, the *Toonerville Trolley*, was in contemporary newspapers of the time. The skipper of the trolley always had a gag line, good for a chuckle. I had a cardboard replica of the Trolley when I was five and assembled the cutout to form a three three dimensional vehicle.

A prominent advertising cartoon appeared on the billboards at the elevated train stations in New York City, showing an oversized mosquito ready to attack a victim, and the quote, "Quick Henry, the Flit!" Flit was a commercial insecticide. That cartoon probably launched the career of the originator, Theodore Geisel. He subsequently wrote many popular children's books under his better-known name, Dr. Seuss.

NIGHT FIRE

One night, Mother jarred my younger brother and me out of bed from a sound sleep. Her rapid talk reflected her fear. "Quickly, children, outside!" she said. Puzzled, wondering why we were herded outside at night, yet still not fully awake, we complied. I saw tall orange flames nearby on our street. The smoke that drifted toward us made me cough. Fire engines clanged in my ears. I shivered from fear, but mostly from excitement. Next day I understood why Mother had been frightened. Our house and the two houses between Meyerowitz's and ours were wooden and close to one another.

In the morning I walked down the street toward the scorched remains of the Meyerowitz house. I had a feeling that I was not supposed to be there, so I was hesitant when I climbed the stone steps to the first floor. Mother's fears had infected my consciousness, but often I rebelled and refused to respond to her concerns. I had an independent spirit, but her shadow lingered, barely in the background.

The front of the red brick house was edged with a thin covering of soot. I dragged my forefinger across the brick and looked at the fingerprint outlined in black on my hand. I stepped over the threshold and saw the shiny blackness inside. I was both attracted and repelled by the charred scent remaining from last night's fire.

Even now the smell of char and smoke from a wood fire stirs the memory of that night in Brooklyn and the pungent scent of burned wood in the Meyerowitz house.

PASSOVER

I find it strange that I can't remember Jewish holidays that we must have celebrated with my orthodox grandmother. But my memories are secular. Instead of a religious celebration, I associate Passover with raisins and nuts, especially filberts, a special treat during the holiday.

Boys played banker-broker using the filberts. We scooped out a hole in the dirt strip between the sidewalk and street. We called it a *shim* from *schimmel*, the Yiddish word for hole. The banker was in charge. Each competitor in turn stood behind a line scraped in the dirt six feet from the shim and tossed a fistful of filberts toward the hole. If we got an even number in the shim, the banker paid us with an equal number of nuts. If an odd number fell in the hole, he collected those. The banker kept all the nuts thrown if none entered the hole. If all the nuts fell into the hole, the banker paid a matching amount and the player became banker.

I loved to eat the nuts, and so I always kept some of my supply, even if I lost the rest to the bank. I used to wrap my hoarded nuts in a handkerchief and strike it against the sidewalk or a brick wall to crack the shells and recover the meats. My handkerchiefs became threadbare and full of holes, much to Mother's annoyance.

"How do you manage to wear out your handkerchiefs?" she asked. I had no intention of telling her.

GHETTO DISSONANCE 1933

I hang from my window
devouring delectable sounds
afternoon cacophony
of street pushcarts
    peddlers' "I cash clothes, I cash clothes!"
    peanut vending whistles.

Winter brings
    steaming chestnuts
    hayse arbe, hot chickpeas
Summer brings
Italian ices
vendors with five cent ice creams
not fifteen cent pops
from tidy Good Humor trucks
    luxuries too expensive
for poor immigrants.

CONFINED BY MEASLES

It was summer. Instead of playing outdoors, I gazed out the window on Warwick Street. A spectator, I was confined with my red leopard-like spots. My attack of measles had almost run its course.

We lived between Blake and Sutter Avenues. Blake Avenue was the site of many pushcarts that lined up on the street. Merchants sold clothing, food, kitchenware, and anything that could fit in their carts. They chanted their wares, a cacophony, like symphony players tuning up.

A pushcart peddler cried in his immigrant accent, "I cash clothes, I cash clothes!" His large wagon wheels creaked in tune with his singsong message. He came from the direction of Sutter Avenue. I watched him as he disappeared down our street, and retreated to the gathering of the pushcarts on Blake Avenue.

Still staring out the window with my speckled face, I awaited the next act of the Jewish ghetto. I heard bells. It was the Italian ices man, pulling on the bell-rope and calling out his, "Icey, ices, come-a-getta-you ices." Lemon-a, strawberry, all-a-kinds, lotsa-kinds. Nice-a-fresh ices. Cool-a- you mouth, tasta good."

Boys and girls gathered around his horse-drawn yellow cart. My mouth watered. I remembered other hot July days and I could imagine tasting the refreshingly smooth red, orange, or yellow ices.

"Mom, could you go down and buy some for me?" But she was too busy preparing for Friday night *Shabbes* (Sabath) supper. Besides, she believed that I shouldn't have something so cold because of my illness. Mothers were and are that way. I sighed and thought of winter to cool me off.

Sounds of musical chimes. A Good Humor truck came by, white and tidy with a luscious-looking chocolate-covered ice cream pop painted on its side. These luxuries cost fifteen cents, so he had few sales on this street of poor immigrants. The other vendor would come by soon and sell many five-cent ice creams, but I was still stuck indoors on the second floor. Life had left me behind.

At last I heard the peanut vendor, the high-pitched whistle shattering the air, while the captivating scent of roasting peanuts wafted forth. He was indifferent to the seasons and came by summer and winter. Everybody loved hot peanuts in the shell, whether at the circus or in the neighborhood. "Mom, it's only a nickel a bag. Please, Mom!"

She went out and bought some for me. I tore open the bag and inhaled the warm rich scent. I squeezed the shells between my fingers, peeled the red skins, and happily chewed the crunchy peanuts. Although sick, I felt much better as I gobbled nut after nut, until Mother called out, "No more, Albert, you'll lose your appetite for supper." I quickly gobbled another handful, and went down to supper with my cheeks full, trying to pretend my mouth was empty.

WARWICK STREET REVISITED

I remember a *shul*, Yiddish for synagogue, on Blake Avenue, near Warwick Street. Most of the immigrant Eastern European Jews in this section of Brooklyn were orthodox and many synagogues served them.

Many years later as an adult I visited the street and found the windows of the local synagogue broken, presumably by vandals. Other than old people, most of the Jews had left the area. Young families moved to the suburbs, on Long Island, New Jersey, or Westchester County. In a common progression of the time, African-Americans took their places on Warwick Street. Then the *shul* morphed into a Baptist church for the new arrivals, and the Jewish ghetto became a Black ghetto. I observed that the street was broken, and the pavement began to return to nature, weeds and all. Signs indicated that the streets were under construction, though I saw little activity.

On another visit after some years, I was pleased to see that paving had been repaired, and small two-story garden houses had been built for the poor, a vast improvement over the tall apartment houses, known as The Projects, notorious in Chicago and The Bronx.

END OF A CHILD'S ERA

While reading comics one afternoon, I heard my mother's sudden cry from below. I rushed downstairs. She sent me back up. Grandma had just died. Crying and moaning continued. I began to cry, aware that Grandma's warm lovingness would be no more. Her sweet-sour scent, so familiar, yet so strange, was gone forever. It was the first family death I had experienced. My five-year-old brother was bewildered. "Why aren't you crying? Grandma is dead," I chided. Intimidated, he joined the crying.

The event brought other changes to my life. As long as Bubbe was alive, like other Jewish boys I had go to Hebrew school, *cheder*, to prepare for my Bar Mitzvah. I hated *cheder,* and its tyrannical rabbi, but especially the loss of my free afternoons after public school. And so I was freed from the prison, since Mother wasn't religious, and Dad apparently didn't care. We had a Kosher household but only while Grandma was alive. Mother never liked the idea of *Kashruth*, Kosher, and its strict food rules, but she respected Grandma's and Dad's wishes.

After Grandma died, most trappings of religious observance died with her. However, Dad sat *shiva*, mourning after her death. Also in the tradition, Dad tore part of his clothing and sat on a low stool for a week. He continued to light a candle each year, *Yahrzeit* to commemorate the date of her death. Although I think he was not a true believer in the religion (I never heard him discuss his religious beliefs), as a loving son, he honored her memory.

Grandma's house was inherited by Zeyde, my step-grandfather. We moved shortly after Grandma's death. We had lived on Warwick Street for only two years.

Freed from orthodox rules, we began to eat bacon and eggs. Our meals were much tastier—rare roast beef and crisp vegetables instead of the overcooked foods that followed immigrants across the sea from Eastern Europe, including boiled fish, boiled cauliflower, even boiled chicken.

Mother decided to move us to so-called better neighborhoods when finances permitted, and we had to move downward when finances looked bleak. I would have preferred to remain wherever we were so I could reach equilibrium with my playmates, and perhaps develop some friendships that lasted more than year or two. But at age six, seven or thirteen, I had no vote on the matter.

I don't know how Dad managed the higher rent, but we moved to Kensington, an attractive middle class neighborhood on the edge of Flatbush, not far from Prospect Park. It was a change to a more American way of life, away from the East New York ghetto. We settled on Ocean Parkway, which at the time had a bridle trail close to the front of our apartment house. I was the same age as the other boys there, and no longer at the bottom of a totem pole.

But now I had to live with a critical mother without the leavening of a loving grandmother, my only remaining grandparent. I knew I would miss Grandma and the few Yiddish words of love that I remembered, *Ikh libe mein libene kind*, I love my dear child, bestowed with juicy kisses on my cheek.

VI. OCEAN PARKWAY

MOVING ON

lonely sky, gray sky
gray pervades me
      a siren echoes
my silent wail
the moving van is disgorging
my few possessions
new neighborhood
      new school
fifth in my ten years
new teachers
      new friends?
once again a stranger
what have I left behind?

I stand on a see-saw
straddling the balance point
hard to move forward
fearful I will drop
if I move past the middle.

Years later when separated from my wife, I moved from our house to an apartment, where I could hear the whistle of a train in the town. I wailed within, and the sound brought me back to the mournful fire engine sirens.

PS 179

I sometimes wondered about the 1, 2 and 3 class designations that separated students. "1" was the top group. But why did the schools use 3 for the average and 2 for the slow learners? Did the administrators set it up so that slow learners wouldn't feel stigmatized? Somehow 2 instead of 3 would make them think they were placed just behind the 1 class. If so, it was surprising that the officials believed kids would be fooled by that subterfuge.

I had to register at a new school, an old habit. First I was sent to the "2" class for slow students, since I was new and it was the midst of a term. That lasted for two days. The teacher said, "Albert, read page one in the reader." I fairly skimmed along. I had read much more advanced material years ago. It became obvious that I didn't belong there. I was sent to the 3 class, for average kids. A week later I was promoted to the 1 class. Mr. Davis, a bald man with a halo of gray and a full gray moustache, welcomed me with the news that I would have to make up for my late start by writing eight compositions at home. I wrote them carelessly to catch up as quickly as possible. Mr. Davis grunted at my submissions and slapped red marks on my papers with the comment that they were too short. But afterwards we were off to a better start, and in time I was at the top of the class.

CHERCHEZ LA FEMME

Harvey was the first boy I met in the new neighborhood. His family lived in our apartment house, and they were on welfare, known as "relief" at the time. My parents looked askance at people on the dole, including Harvey's family. As a liberal Democrat and former Socialist, my father supported the idea and legitimacy of welfare. However, as a breadwinner for his family, he was a strong believer in individual responsibility. Though he was mostly unemployed during the Great Depression, he never even considered accepting welfare because of his sense of pride. Instead, he sold various items on the street when he was periodically laid off from his job as dress-cutter.

I had always been a shy kid, especially around girls. But something changed after we moved, at least temporarily. Harvey had a tall, dark-haired girlfriend named Gloria. She was pretty with a strong expressive energy. I promptly replaced Harvey in Gloria's affection, and she became my first girlfriend. Gloria and her older sister Muriel lived in the apartment house next to ours, their windows across the courtyard facing ours. On Saturday nights I looked longingly toward their window where Muriel had a party going on. I wanted so to be a part of it. I could see the dancing couples, while the sounds of music drifted through my open window. I would have yearned for sexy Muriel if I had been old enough to understand what sex was all about.

Gloria later became jealous of my new heart-throb Marjorie, who was as pretty as Gloria and brighter and perkier. I didn't explicitly reveal my attraction to Marjorie. Unlike Gloria, Marjorie and I were promoted to the rapid advance class in junior high school, where she became the editor of our school yearbook.

OUR APARTMENT NEIGHBORS

The League of Nations was created after World War I, predating the United Nations. When people referred to a variety of ethnicities and nationalities, they used the earlier term. In that sense, our apartment house on Ocean Parkway was a regular League of Nations. There were Jews, Irish, Greeks, and Italians, among others. They seemed to be compatible and friendly with one another.

Mother told me that our Irish Catholic neighbor once said, "Rose, I'm so bothered. I use birth control devices. We can't afford another child, but the Church says it's sinful, so I don't go to confession." Instead, Mother became her informal confessor.

THE BIG ONES

Dick was well over six feet and massive, probably close to or exceeding three hundred pounds. His wife was a good match, not quite as large, but at least somewhat approaching his dimensions and weight. She wore a large print dress that further emphasized her size. She was pleasant and friendly, as long as she wasn't tussling with Dick. Though he wasn't unfriendly, his voice was gruff, matching his bear-like stature.

The couple lived above us in the apartment house. If we didn't see them, we surely would have been able to guess their size from the sound of their footsteps—like elephants clomping.

Dick was a train conductor on the New York City-owned Independent subway. To get the job he had to pretend he was Irish. He looked every bit of it, even though both he and his wife were Jewish. Many jobs in the thirties were off-limits to Jews, even some municipal jobs. His family name was Fagan, probably assumed or given by the immigration people, truly an Irish name, in spite of Dickens' *Oliver Twist*. And so he passed the test.

He would come home late at light and the fighting took place. First the drinking began. In that sense he seemed a stereotypic Irish clone. Then a shouting match that escalated in volume. The crash of dishes followed. After some time it became quiet. Perhaps their intense anger transformed into the Sex of the Titans.

OUR "POOR" LANDLORD

He was an overweight man with discolored teeth and artificially tinted, reddish hair, that barely covered part of his scalp. On the first day of the month he appeared at our door to collect the rent. His old brown suit was shiny from age and wear. During those continuing Depression years, he was fortunate to own our apartment house and the adjoining one.

One of our neighbors happened to come upon our landlord in midtown Manhattan. He was sitting on the sidewalk as though crippled, with a pair of crutches at his side and a begging bowl in front of him. We were intrigued. Considering his ownership of at least two apartment houses, what could have possibly motivated his miserly behavior?

THE SUPER AND HIS SIDEKICK

Ratner was the janitor of the apartment house next to ours. He was referred to as the super, or superintendent, the New York euphemism for janitor. "You boys, get away from here!" he would growl. He chased us off if we merely trespassed on the walkway leading to "his" house. Being a janitor was somewhat shameful in our milieu, even at that time when jobs were scarce. Apartment house janitors were usually non-Jews from Poland, Lithuania, or Baltic countries, and not highly regarded. Maybe that's why Ratner, a Jew, was such a surly, disagreeable man.

His sidekick, every bit as hostile, but probably more dangerous, was his dog. I'm not sure the chow had a name, but he had a frightening demeanor and reputation. It has been said that dogs take on the face of their masters, or perhaps the reverse. In their case the resemblance was remarkable. The janitor even wore brown that almost matched his dog's color. They both growled.

Gloria lived in the house that Ratner patrolled, and so I had to see her in neutral territory, in front of my apartment house. Whatever made Ratner the way he was, we kids were just careful to avoid him and his dog.

A delivery truck cruised Ocean Parkway weekly, on the inner street between the bridle path and the sidewalk in front of our houses. Jack, the driver, sold Dugan's bread, doughnuts, and cakes, including whole-wheat items that made Mother happy for their healthful quality. He entertained us boys and girls with his jokes, stories, and sang popular songs like "Red Sails in the Sunset," "East of the Sun and West of the Moon." and in his rich Irish tenor, "When Irish Eyes are Smiling." We were always delighted to hear the bells that announced his smiling arrival.

THE BELT

My brother was an easy and satisfying target. I would hide and jump out suddenly. I planned to scare him, without rousing my parents to hear his crying. Sometimes I succeeded. But he learned how to play the game. This time he howled with all the force his normally quiet voice could muster. My head turned, as I heard Dad walking toward us.

"Did you tease Eddy again?" Dad's face and voice were stern.

"No, he's just a crybaby," I said.

"He did, he did! He jumped out and scared me," Eddy whimpered.

Dad brought me into the bedroom and closed the door. He removed his belt that we called a strap. I shivered and cringed in anticipation as I heard the jingle of his belt buckle. He had never hit me before. He looked at me closely. I shrank back. Our eyes met. I was frightened and failed to see that the grim look on his face had changed to a half-hidden smile and a twinkle in his eye. "Albert, don't bother your brother again." His laughter felt like a hug, as he replaced the belt on his trousers.

Years later I understood that it would have been too painful for him to cause me pain.

Postscript: Dad died over fifty years ago when I was twenty-nine. He was only 51. That caused me pain that tears still don't wash away.

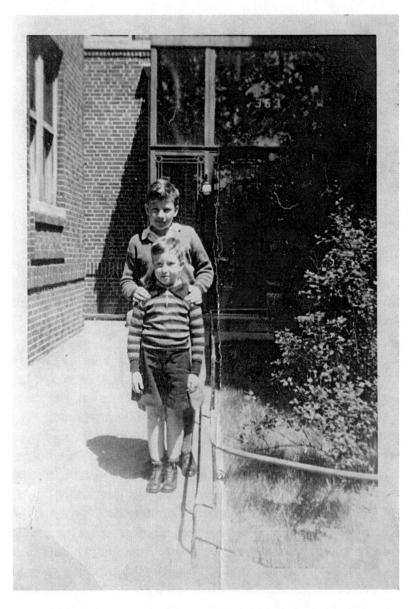

Eddy and Albert, ages 6 and 11 in front of apartment house on Ocean Parkway

A DENT IN THE FENDER

My six-year-old brother's voice often was barely more than a whisper and we didn't pay much attention to what he was mumbling.

The Sears Roebuck deliveryman had carried my new Elgin Bicycle up three stories to our apartment. He stripped off the brown paper covering, revealing a joy to my eye, a shiny bicycle with its red and white frame. Only after the deliveryman left our apartment, did we realize what Eddy had been trying to tell us.

"There's a dent in the fender."

"What?" Mother asked.

Eddy repeated, a bit louder, "There's a dent in the fender."

We looked at the bicycle. There was indeed a dent in the front fender. Sears later replaced the bicycle. But afterward, Eddy continued to communicate softly and we paid more attention to his words, but only part of the time.

Brothers can be so different from one another. In my imagination, I see that double bed we had to share for years, with its brown headboard and black stripe. Yet there was a large gap between us. Eddy is deliberate and speaks precisely. I on the other hand move rapidly, and speak out spontaneously, even carelessly, typical of my impatient personality. I have always been a liberal Democrat like the rest of the family. Although in his teens Eddy was a leftist, later he became and remained a moderately conservative Republican. I received a doctorate and other college degrees. Eddy was and is very bright and would easily have qualified as a student at a first rate university, and probably would have received a scholarship. Instead he chose to attend a two-year course at the Fashion Institute of Technology in New York City. It seemed to fit a pattern. I believe that as second born he had to remove himself from my shadow. He certainly was successful as a vice president of a clothing company.

He lives in Massachusetts, while I am a dyed in the wool Californian. We converse only a few times a year, generally on one another's birthdays. We tacitly and tactfully don't discuss politics, confining our talks to family matters.

MODEL AIRPLANES

As a boy I loved making airplanes. The kits contained balsa wood for the structural members, and thin colored silk-like paper for the skin of the plane, as well as an adhesive to stick the pieces together. It was both a pleasure and a frustration to build a plane. The pleasure was watching the plane gradually take shape as I built up the ribs that formed the fuselage, wings, and tail, and then cementing the paper skin to the skeleton structure. The cement or dope was known as banana oil, a pungent liquid that permeated the air and attracted some "glue sniffers," a dangerous preoccupation. "Banana oil" became a part of the language at the time and often was a response to "applesauce," a term of disbelief like "baloney" or "bullshit." Doubting Thomas might have said "applesauce" to a tale and the response might be, "Oh, banana oil!"

I impatiently waited for each glue joint to dry before trying to cement the whole unit together. If I glued too many joints at once, the unit would fall apart and I'd have to start over. That was one source of frustration. The other was that the cement invariably left spots on the tissue paper skin and on my fingers, which stuck together.

Eventually I overcame my impatience. The pre-formed propeller, its thin hook and the rubber band were connected to the fuselage. If the rubber band was wound too tightly, the plane crushed under the stress and the assembly had to be done again.

At last I was ready for flight. I went out to an empty lot. I raised the plane above my head, held the prop to prevent it from turning, and let go while shoving the plane upward. The plane was supposed to fly. More often than not, it took a nose-dive, smashing into the ground. Back to my workbench, the kitchen table. I could use the table only between meals. Mother chased me off at other times.

I repaired the plane with red silk paper if I ran out of blue. The bicolor plane then looked like my previously torn, patched pants.

Recently on my way to a hike near my home in California, I drove by a launching spot on a hill where men, grown-up boys, were flying their radio-controlled planes. Overhead a model plane dipped and turned at the electronic will of these men, aged thirty-plus. I recalled the model planes of my childhood. No stink of gasoline and exhaust as from these modern planes. No tight control of flight maneuvers, but the quiet joy of buying a kit, building it, and making it fly. The model might have been a copy of a fighting plane from World War I or perhaps one that copied Lindbergh's famed plane, the Spirit of St. Louis.

The radio-controlled planes have the ability to circle, dive, and land, but I had more personal contact with my creations. So what if the flights, when successful, lasted much less than a minute? I would find flying the radio-controlled planes by the hour boring. I wouldn't trade the fun of my model airplanes for today's high-tech planes.

AUTOMOBILES

There were few automobiles in the city during the Depression years. We boys recognized every make and year of Chevvies, Fords, Plymouths, Dodges, and all the others. The unique air-cooled Franklin had a partly leather-covered body. The elegant Cord had a polished metal snorkel for its turbocharger. Cadillac's expensive luxury became synonymous with its name. Uncle Moe usually owned a new Packard, another luxurious car with a vee-shaped front grille that looked as though it could pry open a castle gate. The sumptuous Lincoln was Ford's entry in the expensive parade. The grille of the 1939 Ford looked like a curved, less expensive copy of the Packard's grille. Among foreign cars, Duesenberg stood for German elegance, from which the phrase, "Ain't it a Duesy," was derived, meaning something high class. The Pierce Arrow was another prestigious (i.e., costly) automobile. And very rarely, I would see a Rolls-Royce with its forbidding, in-your-face grille.

In 1938 I saw my first two-toned car, an Oldsmobile. I think it was orange above and tan below, but the exact colors have dissolved in the gray matter of my age. Two-tone was in marked contrast to the Model T. "You can have any color Ford you want, as long as it is black," was said to have been pronounced by Ford, in an unusual reversal of his humorlessness.

Uncle Abe Chasan, Aunt Ada, Elsie, Moe and Sina Freedman
In front: Bob Freedman, me and Dick Freedman

Freedmans—Moe, Sina, cousin Dick

Cousins Elsie Freedman, Eleanor Schwartz, Albert, Dick Freedman

VII. COUSINS, UNCLES, AND AUNTS

I was fortunate to have a profusion of cousins, uncles, and aunts. Years later I learned a Yiddish word that refers to a wider family, *Mishpocheh,* a word that I love to hear and use.

Because I had only a younger brother, I adopted my three male cousins—Bob, Morty, and Sidney as my older brothers. They were five or six years older than I, the same age gap between my younger brother and me.

Bob Freedman was ascetic and I believe not happy with himself. Once when Bob did chemistry experiments at home, he accidentally ground a glass tube into his palm. He dug into hand trying to remove the shards, creating an increasingly deeper hole. He poured iodine into the breech.

Confused about sexuality, as many of us were, he told me that as a teenager, when he had sexual thoughts about a girl, he would imagine she was sitting on a toilet to calm his natural feelings. Oy!

Like a yo-yo he bounced back and forth between Cornell and the University of Chicago. Bob turned to extremes. Religion did not run deep in any of the Chasans, my mother's family and their offspring. Bob's immediate family was also far from observant, but Bob became very involved with Judaism while an undergraduate in college. Later, however, he became a born-again Christian after he married Lucille, the daughter of a minister. She confided in me that his extreme Christianity bothered her.

He was a Republican, and I a Democrat. When I visited him in adult years, he wanted to talk politics. I said, "No, Bob. You know I'm a liberal, and I just want to talk with you as cousins, without politics getting in the way."

In spite of our differences, I loved Bob, and I know that he loved me. His wife told me that he became excited when she picked up the phone and told him that I was calling. But typically, his first words to me were about mathematical problems. He apparently needed to hide from his humanity and love.

Cousin Morty, son of Aunt Sarah and her husband Joe, was much more relaxed when we were together whether we joked, teased, or threw pillows at one another, as I wrote earlier.

Many of my female cousins had names that began with "E," Elsie, Eleanor, Evelyn and Ella and perhaps even my brother Edward, since my mother had expected him to be a girl. More than coincidentally, a Jewish tradition was to name offspring after relatives who had died. My maternal grandmother's name was Elka. She died before my cousins were born.

I regret that I have misplaced a photograph of Ella Priven. She was a beautiful brunette throughout her life. I was pleased and moved when she told me once on the phone years later, "Albert, I always had a crush on you."

When I was a teen, a friend used to call me *Roite*, Red in Yiddish. I didn't understand and objected, but in retrospect, I did have red highlights in my light brown hair and later a reddish beard. My red-haired daughter, Denise and my grandson Albee both have red hair. Three of my cousins, Elsie, Eleanor, and Evelyn were redheads.

My name Rothman translates as red man, which might have been the hair color of an ancestor. Jews were required to take a family name generations ago in Europe. In fact it was not Rothman, my father's name, but it was my mother's side of the family that were replete with blondes and redheads. Originally her family's name was Chasanowitz. When my mother and her siblings were in school, kids distorted the name to Cheese-sandwich. The name was later shortened to Chasan.

Every summer cousin Bob Freedman was sent off to camp. His parents, Sina and Moe were well-to-do and could afford that luxury. Sina had me stay with them for a few days in the summer while Bob was away. They owned a single-family house on a lovely tree-shaded street in residential Brooklyn, an escape away from our apartment. Burning leaves in the fall and new-mown grass in summer perfumed the air. Catkins, that looked like fuzzy caterpillars, fell from the maples in season.

The house had its special scents—-the aroma of food in the kitchen nook, Cousin Elsie's painted masks drying in the finished basement, and the wondrous, slightly musty scent of yellowing book pages in Bob's room.

I slept in Bob's bed while he was at camp. On a shelf above me was a set of ten small, red-bound books entitled *The World's 100 Best Detective Stories.* Other books including Sherlock Holmes, were riches that this ten-year-old boy without an allowance couldn't afford. The place was my haven and magic land. After going to bed I opened a book and gorged myself on the stories until I fell asleep. Next day I awakened to the tempting scent of eggs frying. Aunt Sina called me down to the kitchen, where I devoured the eggs and bacon as I had the stories the night before. If I could locate copies of those little red books now, I would swallow and digest the tales once more.

THANKSGIVING

Because we kept moving, one constant in my life was at Aunt Sina's, where many Thanksgivings were celebrated with the extended family. I had the sense that I was a favorite of Sina.

At our annual Thanksgiving gathering, dinner was a full plate of turkey with the usual trimmings that Aunt Sina, prepared for the larger family with the help of her maid. After dinner, my cousins Bob, his younger brother Dick, Morty, and I played Monopoly in the basement. After the game, I wandered upstairs to see the men.

After dinner the dining table was cleared. The men played Pinochle. Among them were my father and numerous uncles by marriage—Sam, Aunt Minnie's husband with his understated dry humor; quiet-spoken Joe, vivacious Sol, Aunt Esther's husband, among others. They were drinking a bit of *schnapps*, their word for whiskey, one of the few times a year they indulged, always in moderation. I heard what sounded like Ivan pronounced ee-von. Who was this Ivan? I know of none here. As I continued to listen to their game, I realized the word was a play on the word "even," the score in their game.

They teased Bill, the father of Janet, who was married to my cousin Alfred Priven. Bill's wife called him *Volodya,* an endearing name for the Russian equivalent of William. Unlike my own family, Bill and his wife spoke Russian as well as English, perhaps because they had been in the Russian Jewish middle class. The native language of poor Jews in Russia, as my family members had been, was Yiddish.

Bill was an effective goat for the other men, because he easily lost his temper and so the men teased him. His face turned bright red with anger.

Meanwhile the women were in the living room, gossiping or complaining about something or other, probably about their husbands. Harsh-voiced Aunt Minnie, the eldest sister, was the primary complainer.

I took it all in, first listening in at the card game, then I wandered off to the basement with its wonderful paint smell. My cousin Elsie was an art major.

Aunt Sina and husband Moe were the only well-to-do members of the larger family, and the only ones who owned a private house. The rest of us live in rented apartments. Sina was blonde by birth, her hair later assisted by chemistry. An avid and capable bridge player, she aspired to be one of the social set. Moe, a Jew born in England, was a successful businessman, and the only Republican present. He hated President Roosevelt, whom my family adored. Moe spoke freely of his hatred. Everyone else avoided politics in his presence. Uncle Moe had an odd sense of humor. Completely bald, he stood at the head of the stairs, and shouted, "Sina, quick, come here!"

She responded anxiously, "What is it? What is it?"

"Get me a toothpick," he said.

"Why, what's the matter? What's the matter?" she asked.

Moe replied, "I need to comb my hair."

In his comedic way, Moe made fun of the music of Bach. He mimicked the sounds of a violin with "feedle, feedle, feedle!"

Both of Moe's sons had inherited his baldness. Dick the younger one, was called "Puzie," when was a tot. Five years my junior, he died prematurely at sixty. He once recited a ditty, the first line of which rhymed with hell. The second line was:

"….Instead of going to heaven he went to….

Now don't get worried, now don't get pale,

instead of going to Harvard,

he went to Yale."

Dick had sense of humor akin to Uncle Moe's. Dick told about a tailor who had a sign out front, with the words, "I'm Mr. Fink and whadya think? I press your pants for nothing." A customer brought in his pants and when he came to pick them up, the tailor asked for his money. Our protagonist repeated the words on the sign out front. The tailor says, "You didn't read it right. 'I'm Mr. Fink and whadya think? I press your pants for nothing?'" with a Yiddish rising inflection.

Uncle Sol, having had a few drinks began to sing "Sweet Rosie O'Grady," in his Irish tenor voice, though he was as Jewish as the rest of us. Although none of the family was religious, our indelible identification remained as Jews. With his inimitable humor, Moe said it all, "You can change noses, but you can't change Moses."

Aunt Esther was often emotional and could easily begin to cry. Her tears would quickly change to laughter. She was next to the youngest and the most sensitive of the six sisters, a darling woman, full of expressive sentimentality. I've always loved her.

This was but one of our family holiday gatherings that happily resonate in my memory.

Years later I corresponded with Aunt Esther by mail, when we lived on opposite coasts. Her letters were more than literate, and often filled with classical references. She was apologetic about them as though she had nothing interesting to say. On the contrary, I told her how much I enjoyed reading her letters. In high school she had received several awards in English and other subjects, which went unrecognized by Abe, her older brother who acted as the surrogate father for the other seven siblings. I visited her years later, not long before her death. She was quite weak, but happy to see me. I was surprised that she still expressed the pain of her brother's past failure to praise her ability.

Esther had the misfortune to lose one of her two sons, Alan, who died of a heart attack in his thirties. Her husband Sol also died relatively young. It seems she had many issues to cry about.

CHRISTMAS GIFT

A microscope! I loved the gift that Aunt Sina gave me for Christmas. I said Christmas, though we were Jewish. Christmas was a secular holiday for my family, as it seemed to be for many others, especially merchants. My mother and all her siblings were assimilated Jews, perhaps too assimilated.

How magical it was to examine hair, butterfly wings, newspaper print, and anything I could put on the stage of the little microscope. Most wonderful of all were the protozoan creatures I dipped from the ponds in nearby parks: euglena, paramecia, and other fascinating wiggly beasties.

Thanks to Aunt Sina's largesse, the microscope and later her gift of a Chemcraft chemistry set launched me on the way to a love of chemistry and a career in science. Seventy years later I still remember the address of their pleasant home in Brooklyn, 2103 Avenue S. Though Sina and Moe later moved to an elegant house on five wooded acres in suburban Stamford, Connecticut, my memory clings fondly to their previous home in Brooklyn. My mind's eye sees the brick entry to the Tudor house and the driveway between their home and that of the Dorskinds' next door.

Those science sets remind me of another pleasurable toy of my youth—the A. C. Gilbert Erector Set. Sitting on the floor with the pieces spread out before me, I enjoyed building tractors, steam shovels, and skyscrapers from those metal, girder-like pieces that were connected together with screws and nuts. I collected more girders, a motor, and constructed larger structures, until I outgrew childhood and the toy. It would be delightful to build with them now with the same abandon!

UNCLE SAM

"Harry, let's drive to California!" Uncle Sam, was at the wheel of his touring sedan that had mica isenglass windows. He said it to my father, but it was loud enough to be heard in the back seat of the car, where Mother and her sister Aunt Minnie, Sam's wife, were sitting. I was seven years old. We had been driving from a beach in Long Island. Sam and Dad knew that their remark would set off the women to holler, especially Minnie, "No, no, are you crazy?" Although the men were teasing, I would not have been surprised if Sam actually did start to drive westward. He had an adventurous spirit.

The men loved to tease the sisters with outrageous suggestions that they had no intention of carrying out. But it seemed scripted that the women would fall for them and complain loudly.

Minnie was as nervous as a hen in the presence of a fox. She had a high screeching voice and a tic, constantly squeezing both eyes tight. She passed this habit on to Sidney and Alfred, her sons. When I spent time with her, my eyes began to blink in the same way. Mother told me later that Minnie had been a truly beautiful young woman. I found it difficult to believe when she was 60 with her unsmiling wrinkled face and her harsh voice.

Sam was a short, slightly stocky man with full lips and an olive complexion. His dark smooth hair was sprinkled with gray. He had a slow, almost droning voice, and a touch of sly humor accompanied by a barely disguised twinkle in his pale blue eyes. His personality was as different from his wife's as summer is to winter, as day is to night.

My cousin Ella, his daughter, told me that he had escaped from Russia many years before as a stowaway and entered our country illegally, and so he never applied for U.S. citizenship, although he paid Social Security taxes. At sixty-five, he received a Social Security check for six hundred dollars that he returned, believing that as a non-citizen he didn't deserve the money. Twice the check was sent back to him. Twice he returned it. After the third time, he gave up and distributed the money to his three offspring. Sam had a strong sense of integrity and wouldn't keep what he believed didn't belong to him.

Sam ran a small printing shop in the Borough Park neighborhood of Brooklyn. Because of his casual manner and modesty, I hadn't been aware that he had such an excellent command of the English language. He composed text for his clients' advertising, greeting cards, announcements, and the like.

Many years later I visited his shop during my sentimental journey to Brooklyn. An old-fashioned, but serviceable printing press was at the center of the store. Blank papers and cards were carefully filed on nearby shelves. Sam was in his eighties, ready to give up the business. We sat in the shop and talked about the past and the present. For the first time I was able to get close to him, person to person. He complained that few people were using the services of small print shops. He had concerns about the future. In the past he rarely showed his feelings.

When I was a youth at home, my mother was critical of Sam's eating habits. He claimed to eat only pickled herring, salami, and delicatessen generally. To him vegetables were rabbit food. Mother was a vocal advocate of healthful eating of whole grains, vegetables, that is accepted today. She also served plenty of red meat, probably not considered healthful today, but believed to be essential in the 1930's. Her food guru was Carleton Fredericks, a radio personality who promoted healthful foods. Mother was annoying for those who had to listen to her advocate proper foods, as she often did. When she began to preach, my brother and I would sing, "That's what Carleton Frederick says, that's what Carleton Frederick says," to the tune of a singing commercial at that time. She predicted dire things for Sam, based on his bad diet.

Dad died of a heart attack at fifty-one, and Mother died of a stroke at seventy-three. Sam lived on to ninety-two, healthy to the end. He had never gone to a doctor. Sam had led a full life and was ready to let it end. He simply stopped eating.

UNCLE ABE CHASAN

Uncle Abe was Mother's older brother, a man of many talents. Born Abraham Chasanowitz in Russia in 1891, Abe was an excellent mimic. I enjoyed listening to him imitating his Chinese laundryman. "Good...goodgoodgoodgood," spoken with a high-pitched voice. Abe was also superb at imitating Italian and other foreign accents. He was always well groomed and careful in his speech.

He had been allowed to attend free public school in Russia because his father had served in the Czar's army. Public schooling was generally not available to Jews. As a fifteen-year old immigrant to the US, he went to high school like any American. Abe decided to play in a band, but had never studied any instrument. So he bought a saxophone and taught himself to play. He claimed to be a musician, and joined a dance band. I inherited his saxophone that now lies idly in my son's house.

My mother's brothers and sisters, the Chasan family, had lost their father and mother, and Abe as the elder male became the paterfamilias of six sisters and a brother while he held a job during the day. At the same time he was enrolled as an architecture and engineering student at Cooper Union, taking classes at night. Tuition was free for those accepted under that institution's endowment.

In the family dynamics, Abe had his favorites, Sina and Ada. Though Sina wasn't the eldest sister, she became the materfamilias of the brood. Ada was the youngest of the siblings. Rose, my mother, wasn't one his favorites. Their chemistry just wasn't right.

Abe was hired by and designed products for the Otis Elevator Company. The Depression arrived and, like many others, Abe was out of work. He had no regular job for much of that era. He lived in a rooming house in New Jersey, and eked out a living by doing odd jobs as an architect and civil engineer. But pay was minimal.

World War II began. He applied for a job with Westinghouse. Before that time it was generally difficult for Jews to be hired as engineers, so he claimed to be a Christian Scientist of Danish extraction. He could easily pass for a Dane with his light hair, blue eyes and fair complexion. But Westinghouse said they had investigated, knew he was Jewish, and hired him anyway, recognizing his competence and experience at Otis.

Because Abe had spent so much effort raising his siblings, he had no desire to have children of his own, he later told me. In his sixties he married Natalie, who had taken care of her mother and also had never married. They continued to have a twenty-year marriage that worked well for both of them.

I was amused by how this short man drove a car, barely able to see over the steering wheel. "That damned driver, he doesn't know what he's doing!" He half-shouted this over and over as he drove.

"Now, Dear, calm down," Natalie would say. She had a soothing effect on him.

While I was growing up, my mother often used Abe as a censoring figure for me, probably because he had been a critical surrogate father for her. If I got into mischief, she threatened to tell Uncle Abe. He could seem very judgmental, even in his quiet way. I didn't want to incur his displeasure that would spoil my image as a good boy. When he married, I facetiously thought about giving him an Erector set, implying the effect of aging, my passive-aggressive reaction toward him.

Much later, only a year before he died in his eighties, I was fortunate to talk intimately with him. "Uncle Abe, I resented you because you were held up to me as a critic. I'm sorry, and I want you to know that I love you." He also expressed his love for me. We had never spoken of our real feelings to one another before.

Each year Abe and Natalie liked to cruise as passengers in the Caribbean. On his final voyage, Abe went to sleep one night and never awoke. Fate and his sense of responsibility toward his siblings caused him to live a life different from the usual. His talents were also out of the ordinary.

Uncle Lou Chasan and Grandpa Chasanowitz.
Grandpa died before I was born.

UNCLE LOU

Lou was a short, stout, man with full lips. He was almost completely bald. He was Abe's younger brother, and two years younger than my mother. Lou and Mother were close. Uncle Lou acted as my career counselor. Although he had a son and daughter, Bernard and Evelyn, he said that I was like a son to him, to the annoyance of his wife Sally.

I supposedly had a high IQ that Uncle Lou claimed indicated genius. Nowadays we know that IQ is merely a measure of one kind of ability. Lou said, " You can't take credit for being a good student, because it is expected of your high IQ." And so I was in a Catch-22. I could work hard in school and get little credit for personal accomplishment. He also urged me to pursue chemical engineering as a career because he said it yielded a better income than chemistry which I really loved, and so might help me to support my father in the future. My dad died at only 51 and so never needed financial support. My mistake was to listen to Lou whom I admired so much. I didn't really like engineering.

Like his older brother Abe, Lou went to Cooper Union at night to study engineering. During the thirties, he took a job as a teacher, a more stable position, to support his family. When the cloud of the Depression lifted somewhat, he worked part-time on engineering jobs while he continued to teach. By coincidence, he taught mechanical drawing in Montauk Junior High School, where I attended as a student for a few years before high school.

Celia, the mother of Lou's wife Sally lived with them for years. She constantly talked about her weak heart that seemed to be her *shtick*. With their hearty dislike for one another, Lou and his mother-in-law would pass each other in the house, barely acknowledging the person. I wonder if one reason Lou held several jobs at the same time was to avoid contact with his mother-in-law.

He had a sense of humor embedded in a barrage of puns. "Very punny," he'd say about a joke, for instance. Maybe my own sense of puns somehow got passed on through my genes, or perhaps by my affection and admiration for Lou.

Uncle Lou had a desire for adventure. I learned that he wanted to go to California —anywhere but New York. Sally would never hear of it. She didn't want to live far from her grown children. Lou must have been deeply in love with his wife to put up with his dislike of a mother-in-law who lived with them and his unfulfilled wish to live in California.

In my adult years I left a job in California to take a position at Columbia University in New York City. Lou called me aside and said, "Why would you leave California to come out here again?" I realized that my presence in California was a vicarious adventure for him. His death came too early at age 59 in 1957, less than a year before I did return to California for a second and lasting time.

When I hear a recording of piano music by Chopin, I think of Lou. He played piano, and I imagine him playing the music of the composer. When I mentioned my memories of Lou playing Chopin, my cousins Evelyn and Bernard said they had no such recollection. So perhaps it is my imagination, but I cling to my memory, picturing Lou sitting at the piano and hearing him play Chopin compositions.

VIII. JUNIOR HIGH SCHOOL

PS 179 ended in the sixth grade, and so the next step was PS 223, Montauk Junior High School.

My high school and college alma mater tunes were copied from other sources. The words were different, of course. Even my junior high school song "Oh Montauk Junior High School, within your walls sublime dwells a wealth of knowledge and truth," was to the tune of "Old Jeffery Amherst was a soldier of the king…" the Amherst College song.

ORCHESTRA

Our conductor, Mr. Gottlieb, was a temperamental music teacher who seemed to explode when our playing offended him. Anyone who has listened to school orchestras will realize that this could be a frequent offense. He shouted at us when we were off-key or off-rhythm, which was more than occasionally.

I was to play in the orchestra at the graduation of the previous class. I boarded a bus, transferred to another line, and relaxed. I had plenty of time. After fifteen minutes I became aware that the neighborhood looked unfamiliar. I checked with the driver. Oops! I took a bus in the wrong direction. I panicked. How will I make it on time? I debarked, and tapped my foot, waiting for a bus in the opposite direction. I was breathless from panic. Will the bus ever come? Finally it did. Perspiring heavily, both from anxiety and the heat, and breathing hard from rushing from the bus stop, I arrived almost a half-hour late. Fortunately, the event had not yet begun, so all I got was a very unfriendly look from Mr. Gottlieb. It was too public a place for him to shout at me. I took my seat and played.

Since then I have often dreamed of being late, and sometimes

I suddenly look up while I'm driving a car and wonder whether I'm going in the right direction. I have a strange proclivity for being turned around after going to the men's room in a strange building. When I want to leave, I often head in the direction opposite to my destination. Did it all start with that wayward bus? Or was it something built into my baby brain that causes me to take wrong turns?

JUNIOR HIGH KIDS AND TEACHERS

Bobby Blank had dark hair and pale blue eyes, the palest blue I ever remember seeing. I wondered what it would be like to have Blank for a name although he was by no means a blank. Definite and authoritative in his words, he seemed sure of himself, unlike my uncertain self at the time. Unwittingly he left me an unusual legacy, one that was sometimes problematic. When I try to meditate and erase busy thoughts in my mind, I think "blank." But then Bobby Blank comes into mind and undoes my intention!

Mischievous twins Ruth and Eleanor sat in the front row of our English class. Laughingly they told me how they teased the sixty-year old, dirty-minded teacher by crossing their bare legs in class to see the effect on Mr. J. Initially standing, he would sit down behind his desk, perhaps to hide his erection.

Some of the other kids in my class that come to mind are:

Jacqueline K, a brunette pixie, dimpled, cute, and innocently seductive.

Ed Solomon, clear spoken, forceful in his words. I bet that he later became a lawyer. He surely had the talent for it.

Seena Weber, a natural leader with pale reddish-blonde hair, and the palest blonde eyebrows I had ever seen.

Marjorie Schulman, a bright, quick-witted girl, and the editor of the school yearbook. I fell in love with her but I was too shy to tell her. In retrospect I'm sure she knew.

The closest I came to letting her know of my love came

about at a Halloween party. We played "Spin the Bottle." Our bottles lined up and so we went into the next room to kiss. I was about to tell her of my feelings when we were interrupted by her parents' arrival. I think she liked me, because in my autograph book at graduation, she wrote, "Remember the Halloween party?" It was up to the boy to make the first move and I failed the test because I feared the possibility of rejection.

Bernice was one of Marjorie's friends and also an editor of the school's doings. At the time I thought of her as unattractive—a lean face, kinky hair and eyeglasses. Like Marjorie, her repartee was both quick and clever. She must have been bothered by my insensitive remark, calling her fish-face, but she never showed signs of a reaction. In retrospect, I realize that she was an attractive girl. Oddly, a recent comic strip, "Luann," by Greg Evans shows a girl named Bernice with wiry hair and glasses. Could I have anticipated his cartoon?

I displayed even greater insensitivity while with a group of friends. I happened to notice that one of the girls had a faint moustache. It surprised me and without thinking, I loudly called attention to it. When she began to cry, I realized my gaffe and felt guilty about it. In retrospect, I feel embarrassed now by my lack of sensitivity at the time. Even now my words often spill out spontaneously, but I try sometimes without success to avoid offending others.

TUSSLE WITH A BULLY

After class one afternoon a toughie came up to me in the schoolyard and shoved my hat off. Without thinking, I challenged him. I said, "What do you think you're doing?" Again, my spontaneous reaction. He started to swing at me. I fell to the ground to protect myself from getting knocked down. My eyeglasses fell off, and I punched him from below. I took quite a few blows, but later I was proud that I had hit him a few times from my horizontal position, before a teacher stopped the fight.

My friends later asked me whether I was trying to get killed. Didn't I know that the bully carried a knife and had been in reform school? But my testosterone kicked in or I just didn't think before I spoke. Maybe it was the same pattern as when I was four and taunted fat Solly and he beat on me, my love affair with danger.

SOME OF THE TEACHERS

Our English teacher, Mr. J, presented a very proper image. He was middle aged, but he looked older with a prominent whisky nose. He was tall, slim, nattily dressed, had an abnormal fondness for thirteen-year-old nubile girls. Bosomy Miriam R asked him for some literary information after class. He put his arm around her and spoke while she innocently looked up to him. Innocently? Perhaps. Boys asked me why I didn't take advantage of her obvious crush on me. "After all," they said, "she has big tits." But she was too saccharine for my taste.

The scuttlebutt was that Mr. J went down to the basement before class to have a nip with the janitor. Licorice-flavored Sen-sen failed to cover his boozy breath. He once criticized an Italian-American boy. "Why aren't you smart like the Jewish students?" That offensive remark made us Jewish kids wince with embarrassment.

Our eighth grade science teacher was-white haired Mr. Conrad. His hillbilly accent seemed out of place in Brooklyn. He pronounced "tremendous" as "tremenjous." With his glasses below the bridge of his nose, he held a large model, a cross section of a carrot. He nested it in his left arm while pointing to the parts with his right hand. To thirteen-year olds with raging hormones, the giant carrot suggested an overdeveloped penis. When he talked about the tip being hard, snickers filled the room.

He shouted angrily, "Shame on you and your dirty minds!" We cast our eyes down and tried to hide our giggles.

My Latin teacher, Mr. S, relished his subject, saliva drooling as he talked. A kindly man, he was large in height and girth and had an effeminate, high-pitched voice. Thinking back, he seemed like a large eunuch.

I had three and a half years of Latin, for no good reason other than I was under the false impression that it would be useful for a scientific career. German or French would have been more useful. It was my curse to receive good grades in Latin, though I never cared for the language. I disliked its complex noun cases and verb forms, many of which were irregular. I had no patience for the word order, so different from that of English and seemingly so arbitrary. How did the poor Catholic prelates manage to speak Latin, and how did the original Romans themselves? In spite my feelings about the language I was chosen to participate in a city-wide Latin competition. Unsurprisingly, I didn't even come close to winning.

The same toughie with whom I had a one-sided fight after he knocked my hat off in the schoolyard, tried to wise-ass his way in the gym class. Our gym teachers were two tough Irishmen, Mr. O'Connor and Mr. McKenna. They expected us to behave and toe the mark. The bully sassed the teachers. O'Connor took him into an adjoining room and closed the door. We heard whimpers and wails, and the sniveling fellow emerged. We guessed that he'd gotten a beating. Presumably O'Connor put boxing gloves on both of them and proceeded to box with the student. Needless to say, I received much pleasure from the event. Of course, teachers no longer can get away with beating up a kid, even a tough one, but that was in a more wild and woolly era. Maybe those two teachers nowadays might be known as the Irish Mafia.

THE LIBRARIANS

We had several teachers in the school library class. Mrs. Walsh was a beautiful blonde, proud of her Irish ancestry. She characterized herself as having a peaches-and-cream complexion, and she certainly had that. Slender, stylish, with a mellifluous voice and manner, she was a delight. I think "good cop, bad cop." The opposite of sweet and kind Mrs. Walsh, Mrs. X (or was it Miss?) grumbled at us, complaining about how we mistreated library books, not returning them on time, and on and on. I never saw her smile. She told us ominously about "dog-ears," that is, folded-down corners of pages. She made it sound like a deadly sin. Her message was effective for me. I never bend down pages of books, even those that I own. Occasionally I find a library book with some pages folded. I wince, grumble, make a severe judgment about the selfish lout who did the deed, and straighten the page. Ms. X lives on in me.

CHICKEN POX

It was only two weeks to graduation from junior high. What an ironic time to come down with chicken pox!

I gazed out the window, my face smeared with Vicks Vaporub, the medicated salve, to keep the pustules soft and help heal them. Mockingly, that same Vicks now serves to dull the more-than-occasional ache of arthritis in my spine!

"Don't scratch or rub them, Albert. You'll leave a scar," Mother said. They itched, and I tried not to scratch them. I didn't want to end up with holes in my face. But to speed up the healing process I rubbed them, thinking that I could slough them off without leaving pockmarks. I hated the thought that Marjorie would see me with ugly pockmarks on my face.

The pages on the calendar were swallowed rapidly, like desserts at a feast. My photograph was already in the yearbook, and I didn't want to miss my first graduation, only a week away.

A day before graduation, I rubbed out the last three vestiges of my disease. Mother was right. Several small pockmarks remained on my cheek and forehead for years. But at least I was able to attend the ceremony.

Now if only I had dared to approach Marjorie and tell her about my feelings for her. Subsequently we went to different high schools. Once after graduation I knocked on the door of her parents' home to ask her to go bicycle riding with me. Marjorie wasn't at home. I never tried again. I couldn't chance rejection.

Where are you now, Marjorie, more than sixty years later?

BLOSSOM BLOSSOMS

Blossom Link had been in my Latin class. She excelled in the subject, and so was the teacher's favorite. When barely in her teens, she had been skinny and rather plain.

One summer evening, a few years after junior high, I saw a group of boys at an outdoor gathering place on Ocean Parkway. They surrounded a stunningly pretty, sexy young woman, who wore an angora sweater that enhanced her figure. Rather, she enhanced the sweater. I looked closely. It was Blossom. What a transformation! The butterfly had emerged from her cocoon. I couldn't tear myself away, but the competition was too strong. She seemed to gorge herself on the attention. Wonderful what hormones can do! I doubt that she enjoyed Latin as much as the attention of boys drooling over her. And who could blame her?

IX. GATHERINGS

BOYS AND GIRLS TOGETHER

Not, as the song goes, "Me and Mamie O'Rourke," but me, Tom, Dick, Fleur, Beverly, and Margot. And not "The Sidewalks of New York," but Ocean Parkway with my companions.

My friend, and my cousin in-law, Dick, was tall, dark, somewhat handsome, and never seemed to be without a girl friend. He had a teasing sense of humor. Beverly was a cute, petite girl who seemed not to have it all together. Dick pointed up to a distant street-light and convinced Beverly that it was the moon. "Really?" she asked.

"Sure," was his rejoinder. She apparently accepted Dick's word. Did she really believe him? Was she really so stupid, or was she playing her own game on Dick?

Fleur had a breezy way about her. Tossing her head, she acted the pretty lady. Her complexion was like a fresh peach, and she always seemed newly scrubbed, as if she had just emerged from a bath. Her boyfriend Bill was a handsome blond who lived a few blocks away. He apparently had more than one girlfriend, and that created a problem.

On Valentine's Day, Fleur opened a letter from Bill that clearly had been directed to Susan, his other girl. I assumed that Susan received a similar valentine intended for Fleur. The envelopes were addressed correctly, but he had inserted the wrong valentine in each. He managed to charm his way back to Fleur. I wouldn't be surprised if he grew up to be a super-salesman.

We referred to Margot Lipiner as a refugee, that Jews were called who fortunately escaped from Germany before Hitler had activated the final solution, the euphemism for extermination of the Jews.

Her flushed face broadcast Margot's emotions, especially when she was embarrassed or angry.

She was an intelligent girl with pale blonde, almost strawberry-colored hair and eyebrows and had a barely detectable German accent. I think we were strongly attracted to one another that neither of us ever expressed. I liked her intelligence, and I think she liked mine. I wonder what would have happened if I had awakened to that attraction and spoken to her about it.

Sic transit gloria, or rather Margot.

Girls often walked together, arms locked, singing the popular songs of the time. The words were printed weekly and were available at newsstands. At times the girls would humorously twist the words. "When the swallows come back to Capistrano," became "When the swallows come back for hot pastrami."

Boys, on the other hand, sang old standby songs such as "Donderbecker, Donderbecker, how could you be so mean, for ever inventing a sausage meat machine? Now all the rats and pussycats will never more be seen. They'll all be ground to sausage meat in Donderbeck's machine." Stanza after stanza continued until we got tired. We also had some songs like "I used to work in Chicago in a department store, but I don't work there no more," that also had many stanzas, most of which would be x-rated.

A COLLECTION OF BOYS

Sumner Radler! I never thought much about it then, but the name seems like one invented in Hollywood or from a boy's adventure book, but he was a real person. Sumner's loose brown hair bounced as he strutted along in the neighborhood. He walked jauntily, raising the heels of his sneakers high with each step. We used to call one who walked that way a "hot guy," cocky and egotistical. But Sumner was much more than that. He was good-natured.

One day Sumner was walking along, helping himself to candy from a white bag. I appeared from around the corner. "Would you like some?" he asked invitingly, holding the open bag toward me. I said no. He responded "Thanks!" and breathed a sigh of relief, showing both his generosity and ambivalence about sharing the candy.

He was a good handball player, a *de rigueur* game in the schoolyard. The court was marked with chalk, and we played the ball against the cement wall of the school. I once beat him in a game, or maybe it was a draw. Perhaps my pride prevents me from remembering the truth. But I think the name Sumner Radler is almost a rhythmic mantra, never to be forgotten.

Arnie D, a boy with smooth dark hair and a surgically repaired harelip. Mothers placed him off-limits to neighborhood boys. Not by mine, because I moved into the neighborhood after Arnie returned from reform school.

According to my new companions, some boys had thrown rocks that broke the few remaining windows of an empty house on Ocean Parkway. While they were busily hurling rocks, a policeman arrived, called by some neighbors. The kids scattered, all but Arnie. He was so intent on the task at hand that he kept on throwing. He paid the price for all of them. It seemed unfair. Maybe that's why Arnie appeared bitter at times. I liked his spirit and we got along well.

A boy with the same first name was Arnie C. He was eleven, a year younger than me. We native Brooklyn boys thought he spoke with a strange accent, since he was originally from Erie, Pennsylvania. He pronounced a release of wind as fart. We Brooklyn natives knew the right pronunciation was fot. It wasn't till I left my native borough that I learned that his pronunciation was the correct one. He had a nasty habit of picking his nose and giggling as he put his finger in his mouth. Yuk!

Arnie had a naïve view of sex. "You mean to tell me my father would do *that* to my mother? I don't believe it," said Arnie. I could almost agree. His mother seemed sexless to me, even though I was only twelve.

"Where do you think babies come from, Arnie?"

"Well, certainly not in that dirty way," he answered.

Often he was our patsy. Three of us—Arnie, our friend Bert, and I went to a Saturday matinee and saw "San Francisco" and "A Night at the Opera", with the Marx Brothers. Bert and I played a trick that boys often did at that time. We tried to flip open Arnie's fly. In those days flies were buttoned, not zippered. While dodging us, he ran in front of a moving bus, and was grazed. We had the uncomfortable task of reporting the event to his mother. Fortunately, his injury was only slight. But the fly game lost its zest.

CALL ME THOMAS BELFAST

Tommy Cohen was one of my neighborhood acquaintances. Tommy fell in the crack between Jew and Gentile. His father was Jewish, his mother Irish. To avoid being one of the disliked minority, Tommy assumed his mother's maiden name and called himself Thomas Belfast. He took on the air of an Irishman, and developed a brogue that authenticated his choice of ethnicity and escaped his Moses identity. Eventually Cohen separated from the rest of us, and Belfast joined the informal Brooklyn Irish brigade.

LARRY HABER

He had a cherubic face. By a felicitous error I typed "cheerubic," an appropriate description of Larry. He would swing by with his dark curly hair and his chubby dimpled cheeks. He looked like a boyhood version of Babe Ruth, the baseball hero. Larry was big and had a rotund face like The Babe. There the resemblance ended. I don't recall broad smiles on the Baseball Great, who often seemed dour. On the contrary, Larry had a perpetual smile and laugh.

He seemed to be a foolish clown. But in our unexpressed adolescent way, we enjoyed his laughter. Larry reflected an upbeat optimism, even in those early teen years that most of us took so seriously.

I wonder how his life evolved. A half-century's gap and continent's width away are chasms too wide to breach. I hope that his cheery manner stayed with him.

THE UNTWINNED TWINS

Two of my friends were Johnny and Artie, identical twins, a few years my senior. They looked like one another, and even dressed alike. But there the similarity ended.

Johnny, a relatively quiet and modest man worked as an electrician at the Brooklyn Navy Yard. Artie, more outgoing than his brother, had many adventures and positions, if you were to believe him. And that was the rub. Eventually I realized that his tales were fabricated. There were too many of them that did not fit what I knew, and so I didn't believe any of them.

One day I told him I had been hiking in the Palisades. "Oh yes, I've been there many times," he said.

"How did you get there?" I asked.

"I took the train," said Artie. Unfortunately, no train went close to the place. One had to take a bus across the George Washington Bridge.

If I said I had seen a movie, Artie had supposedly had seen it before I did, sometimes even before the film had been released! I was reminded of Baron Munchausen, the fictional figure whose exploits were largely imaginary. I'm not sure of what Artie did for a living, because he was armed with his smoke screen.

I suppose Artie needed to invent himself because he doubted his worth. However, I liked him and continued to be his friend. At first I questioned him, but after awhile I simply nodded, as if to agree. I suppose he didn't realize that he was liked just for himself and needed no amplification to be accepted.

BOHEMIA-HO

In my teen years, I found it exciting to be with other guys, walking the street together at night, swinging our arms, singing in loud voices, and feeling a sense of comradeship. One such group of boys called themselves a fraternity. They were in one sense of the word, though not like a formal college-type fraternity. The boys sang songs like "Bohemia-ho, Bohemia-ho, where every man is king." I had never heard these songs before, but it was so much fun to belt out with other fellows. Unfortunately, it was to be a one-time event for me. I longed to join them, but they met in the evening on the street and exacted a nominal fee—for what, I can't imagine. But my mother, without giving a reason that I can remember, said "No." I had no money of my own.

She did the same when I wanted to join the Boy Scouts. They also charged a modest fee. I deeply wanted to become one of them, learn to tie knots, and enjoy the outdoors. She may have been convinced by her brother, my Uncle Lou, who believed that the Scouts were militaristic, likely because of their uniforms. She later relented and allowed my younger brother to become a Scout. He ultimately advanced to be an Eagle Scout. Although I never mastered knots, I learned to guide myself in the wild. I was drawn to the outdoors like a magnet attracting a compass needle.

In retrospect I believe Mother did what she thought was best for me. But she was an insecure, frightened woman, in part because of her childhood in Russia, and so she gained a measure of control by trying to control me. When I asked for an allowance that other kids had, her response was, "Just ask me if you want something." I would add parenthetically to her unspoken words, "*If* I want you to have it."

OUTDOOR ADVENTURE

Even as a child this city boy was partly conscious of an inchoate longing for adventure. The closest I came was to ride my Elgin bicycle far and wide on Brooklyn streets at age twelve. In high school I sat on the roof of my apartment house to do my schoolwork, to read, to gaze at the clouds, and to feel the wind.

My first real outing was with boyhood friends who formed a club, bought knapsacks, and went by bus to Palisades Park in New Jersey to camp. The park was on a level forest at the top of a cliff that leads down to the Hudson River. Camping for us consisted in building a fire and feasting on Heinz baked beans, then returning home. But for me this was an adventure away from the city, that reasserted itself when I became a hiker and lover of nature many years later.

MY FRIEND NORMAN

Norman was homely, with a sunken chest and a large bulbous nose. His straight blond hair flapped loosely in the wind. Unlike my father, a working man, his father was a professional, an optometrist and bank examiner.

Norman and I had both complementary and overlapping interests. Norman's were in electronics, photography and machine shop. Mine were in chemistry and science in general. I learned photography from him and he learned chemistry from me. His family lived in a private house, where he had the run of his basement—his workshop and our chemical laboratory. There I could do chemical experiments that I couldn't do in the apartment house we lived in. Norman also had a substantial money allowance that helped both of us, since I had none.

Our personalities were very different. He was mostly wrapped up with his shop tools or camera equipment, while I socialized at times with boys and girls.

On some weekends Norman's family chose to drive to a Long Island beach and wanted him to go along. Norman refused, preferring to stay in his workshop. He didn't like the beach and wanted to spend as little time as possible with his family. Father and son then got into a shouting match. I would have been happy to go to the beach. Unlike Norman, I loved the outdoors, and my family had no car to go to distant Jones Beach, unattainable by public transportation. Norman won the round, and so neither he nor I got to the beach that day.

Norman's eating habits were unique and unhealthful. He loved "Pabst-ett," a processed cheese that he smeared generously on white bread, that seemed to be his dietary mainstay.

He hated onions, especially raw, another source of disagreement in his family. From his basement shop he would suddenly bolt up the cellar stairs toward the kitchen and slam the door forcefully. A frequent scene then played out. His overweight, henna-haired mother would open the basement door and shout, "Are you crazy?"

Norman's loud response was to complain about the stink of onions cooking that she denied in spite of the obvious odor.

"Close the damn door!" Norman would yell, and the fight continued. I remained a silent, innocent bystander.

Sometimes I suggested, "It's a nice day. Let's go for a walk." He demurred. He was happier in his basement and saw no point in walking, unless he had a specific destination, and then he would prefer to use his bicycle. He usually had a black bicycle clip on the right leg of his trousers, ready to ride someplace if necessary.

His eating habits eventually caught up with him years later. He died of a heart attack at age sixty.

He often answered facetiously to my serious questions. His odd humor extended to other matters. For example, if he saw me a block away, he would shout, "Al, come here, quick!" I would rush over, thinking it was an emergency. When I reached him he would say, "Where would you be if you hadn't come?" I was mildly annoyed. Of course his gambit no longer worked after the first few times.

He had some expressions that I don't recall hearing anywhere else. The one that comes to mind is "as pointless as a pretzel," referring to a story that made little sense to him.

Norman's father was slight, much shorter than his abundantly large wife. He had a pencil-thin moustache and narrow slits for eyes, both of which fit his insidious personality. He often wore an armless undershirt in the house and owned dirty pictures that we found in his bureau and enjoyed with our adolescent lust. Mr. T had the unpleasant habit of goosing me and other friends of Norman and even grabbing at our genitals. Once, with a lecherous look on his face, he insinuated, "Al, you know your mother is a very attractive woman." I was embarrassed, but I didn't know what to say in response. My mother actually was pretty, and certainly compared to his wife, who had coarse facial features that were duplicated somewhat on the faces of Norman and his older sister.

Norman and I enjoyed many activities together, including bits of mischief. One day we rigged a water sprayer, consisting of a large jug of water and an air pump. We chased some kids who were annoying us. While running we pumped and sprayed water a distance of thirty feet, thoroughly dousing them.

We had fun indoors, too.

Norm played harmonica and convinced me to buy one. The best ones were made in Germany. I didn't stop to think about that when I bought my harmonica. My father was upset when he learned about the purchase. "Here I am contributing to anti-Nazi organizations while you bought a German product." The Nazis, of course, were persecuting and later murdering Jews. I felt guilty. I had let my father down, even though I had done so unintentionally.

Norman and Albert Sweet Adelining
Photo by Norman

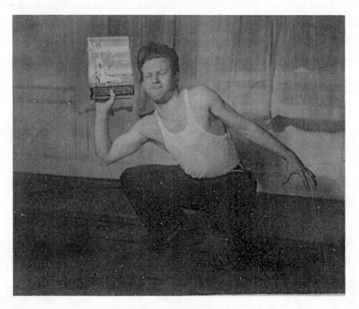

"Heavy literature"
Photo by Norman

Later that year, I had to sit up in the front row of the class to see the blackboard. I reluctantly decided that I needed glasses. Pride prevented me from wearing them outside of school. Norman's father, an optometrist, believed that wearing glasses continuously would weaken my vision. Since then I have learned that it was an old wives' tale, or rather an old optometrist's tale. One advantage, however, was that I learned to recognize friends by their shape and stance even at a distance, a technique that I have continued to use.

One day Norman, his sister, and his father were in his backyard. They looked up, laughed, and pointed to a third floor window of an apartment house. A nude woman was standing at the window. She became aware of being on display, and quickly drew the shade. I missed out on the treat because of my uncorrected myopia. From then on, I decided to wear my glasses more often.

Sometimes there were four of us in an informal club—

Norman, in whose basement we convened, Myron, a quiet classmate of mine whom I knew from junior high school, and I the chemist who set the agenda. Finally, there was Dick, seemingly narcoleptic. He sat on a high stool, and nodded off regularly, like the dormouse in *Alice in Wonderland.* Dick was easy-going and didn't seem to mind being teased about constantly falling asleep.

We sat around in the basement, surrounded by Norman's prize tools—his lathe, drill press and several photographic enlargers. Norman got most of the material things that he wanted and let me share his "toys." My family, on the other hand, barely had enough for a hand to mouth existence. Food and rent and occasional clothing saturated the sponge of our income. I had few possessions. Although our family was not perfect, I had a warm, understanding dad in contrast to Norman's difficult father.

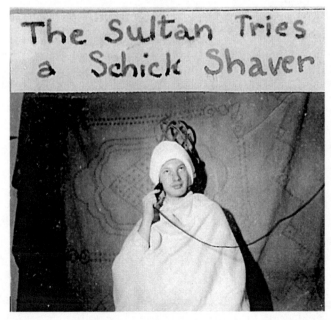

No longer a little shaver.
Photo by Norman

EXPLOSIONS

I had been intrigued by the thought of preparing a mild explosive, nitrogen tri-iodide, in Norman's boyhood basement. I had heard that mischievous boys would coat a doorknob with the wet chemical, and allow it to dry. Turning the knob to enter the room, the unwary would be surprised by the loud "pop" of the explosion.

It is a simple chemical to prepare: mix iodine crystals with ordinary household ammonia, then filter the material. While Dick snored an obbligato, the rest of our foursome prepared the Devil's brew, and each of us laid the moist compound on shallow concave dishes known as watch glasses, and left them to dry overnight.

The next day we were surprised to find that several of the glasses had shattered. Who said the chemical had to be touched to explode? Evidently even air motion was enough to detonate it. We used a feather to touch the few glasses that were still unbroken and saw small explosions and puffs of violet smoke, as the nitrogen iodide decomposed to nitrogen and iodine vapor.

Fortunately we didn't prepare a massive amount of the iodide, or the tale might have had a dismal instead of gratifying finish.

Once I learned that a man was disposing of his whole chemical laboratory. We, or rather Norman, would buy some of the things. Unfortunately I mentioned it to my Cousin Bob Freedman, who had a large allowance from his wealthy family. Before we could offer to buy a few of the chemicals and glassware, Bob bought the whole shebang for himself. He never shared any of the items with us, a selfish side of Bob I hadn't realized before, but I continued to love him.

A German-Jewish refugee family that had escaped Hitler lived next door to Norman's house. The father, Mr. G, was a pompous know-it-all; Germanic stubbornness had rubbed off on him. He insisted that the Roman Caesar was pronounced Tsayzar in Latin. In my Latin class we learned that the pronunciation was Kyssar. But Mr. G persisted in his opinion, that was likely based on how one would pronounce it in the German language. His son Werner was happy-go-lucky, laughed a lot, and seemed like a fool. Werner's sister Ilse sometimes sat on Norman's lap and allowed Norman to play with her breasts, that we called feeling her up. I envied Norman. I would have loved to fondle a girl in that way.

Once Norman and I found an old phonograph record of "Valencia" in his house. We listened to it, enjoying the wobbly words and music on this old gem.

Years later, my wife and I moved to the San Francisco region. Norman and his wife Ruthe happened to move there a few years later. Norman filled the living room in their newly-bought house with four photographic enlargers and several lathes and other shop tools, far more than he could use. It was like a reenactment of his boyhood, but with many more material things. He also had a large garage built, not for his car, but for his oversupply of tools, photographic equipment, and other grownup toys. After Norman's death, Ruthe took several years to sell all his accumulated equipment.

BICYCLE ADVENTURES—FOUND AND LOST

The colors! The textures! The angular crystals! How could I resist? I heard about a mineralogy class at the Brooklyn Children's Museum, and decided to sign up. There were not many choices for a boy to enrich his summer. I wasn't aware of any free public swimming pools in our neighborhood.

I could get to the museum by bus, but that would require hours for the trip—catch a bus, then wait to change to other buses. Instead I got there by pedal power in less than an hour, on my shiny red Elgin bicycle. The treasured bicycle carried me all over Brooklyn. This Lone Ranger experienced many different neighborhoods.

On a sunny Tuesday I rode up Cortelyou Road past the tidy houses on Clarendon. After a few more miles I cycled to New York Avenue past Eastern Parkway and turned right on Park Place to the museum. The neighborhood was known as Brower Park, innocent in name only. It was next door to the Bedford-Stuyvesant area, notorious for poverty and crime.

I parked the bike outside the museum, chained the frame and rear wheel to the picket fence, and danced inside to learn about minerals. In the class I learned about the Moh's hardness scale, and began to identify minerals by crystal shape, color, and hardness. I left with mimeographed sheets. The sketches were in black and white, but I remembered the beautiful colors and shapes of the minerals. At home I lapped up the information, like a dog drinking from a bowl of milk.

I repeated the round trip journey on my trusty wheeled steed on Thursday.

On the following Tuesday, once again I made the trip to the museum. After I left the class, I approached my bicycle. It was now a monocycle. My front wheel was missing, stolen in this seedy neighborhood. What should I do? I walked to a phone booth and phoned Uncle Lou, who owned an automobile. He picked me up, put the crippled bicycle, in his car and drove home. My family bought me a new front wheel. But discouraged, my enthusiasm had chilled, and I gave up my mineral pursuit. Too bad, since I loved the forms and colors of nature's gems.

That wasn't the end of my cycle's victimization. My bicycle must have had bad Karma. A few years later, while visiting my friend Norman, I parked my bicycle in his side yard, leaning it against the house as I usually did. While inside, I heard the ring of my bike's bell, and assumed my friend Dick was announcing his presence. When nobody appeared, I looked outside and my bicycle was fast disappearing down the street. Norman's father got into his car and drove me on Ocean Parkway, trying to follow the purloined wheels. We turned up Eighteenth Avenue where we last caught sight of the fleeing thief. The chase was hopeless. We saw the crook enter a small apartment house. We knocked on the door, and were confronted by an innocent looking boy, who said, in answer to my question, "What bicycle?"

Friends later told me that a family of thieves lived in the house. They'd been known to steal bicycles, carry them up to the roof, repaint and sell them later on the hot market. My family couldn't afford to replace the Elgin. That was the demise of my trusty bicycle and the end of riding the Brooklyn streets. By this time I was busy in high school studies, and so I followed other pursuits. But I never completely got over the loss of my rolling friend.

X. THE UNEXPECTED HERO

Wild about Harry

With the possible exception of those who have brutal fathers, our dads are our heroes. Who better to look up to when we are released from our mother's apron strings?

My father was a short, unassuming man with dark curly hair. He was kind both to his boys and his wife's relatives. He had a rather ironic sense of realism about the world, but he was not cynical.

When I was four or five I felt happy walking with Dad, my small hand grasping one of his smooth, large fingers. He moved slowly, so as not to outpace my small steps. We played a kind of baseball together. How proud I was when Daddy's bat hit the soft rubber ball well over my head. I believed that he was the strongest, most powerful man alive. Did others even come close?

Another pleasant memory was his unshaven face. It was comforting to feel the roughness of his day-old stubble against my smooth young face.

We grow older and become both wiser and yet often more foolish. In my teen years, I copied my mother's attitude and became critical of Dad. He used to listen to WEVD, the Yiddish radio station. I wanted to be American, and was ashamed of the Old World language.

I always knew Dad loved, cared for, and accepted me just as I was. Only when I matured did I understand just how tender and caring he was. He didn't express his love in words. It was typical of men in those days, and it seems to be true for many men today.

I love to feign a so-called Yiddish accent, or more accurately, an Eastern European Jewish accent, maybe because I regret my early wish not to be a Jew, and seek some connection with both my father and my Jewish heritage .

Though Dad had a strong native intelligence, he had very

little formal education—a year or two of night school in his twenties after he emigrated from Russia. Mother insisted on it as a pre-condition for marrying him. He had missed a chance to go to school in Russia, because he had to support his widowed mother. Yet he could do complex mathematical calculations in his head. Once I showed him the power of algebra to solve a mathematical problem. "Show me the problem," Dad said casually. I did, and he solved it in his head using ordinary arithmetic and reasoning. I learned later that as a dress cutter, not often thought of as a prestigious job, he had to calculate the best fit for cutting a pattern of many dresses in a machine, to minimize loss of costly material.

At my high school graduation in Carnegie Hall I was called up to the stage five times to receive awards in various subjects—including chemistry, English, math, and others. My mother, sitting next to him, told me later that he wept with pride and joy.

Dad would discipline me verbally, but he never hit or even slapped me. He was at ease equally with men and women, in an era when many men felt uncomfortable talking to women. Consequently, women found him endearing. But in addition to his sensitivity and openness, this unassuming man was also a hero in his matter-of-fact way.

We lived in an apartment house on Ocean Parkway in Brooklyn as I mentioned before. The parkway has a central highway where cars moved rapidly. Pedestrian benches were set in cement next to a paved bicycle and walking path.

Ruth was a divorced mother with her three-year old son Charles. One day Dad, Ruth, and I were sitting on a bench and chatting. Suddenly, Charles ran out into the highway. Without hesitation, Dad jumped up and ran after the boy. He tried to halt traffic by waving as he ran. Fortunately he succeeded, scooped up Charles, and both returned safely. He and the child could easily have been struck and killed.

My brother told me about another of Dad's deeds. Eddy

and Dad were walking together in a seedy neighborhood. In a side alley a man was attempting to rob another while using a knife as a threat. Dad rushed over, shouted, "Stop that!" and chased the would-be robber away. Harry Rothman was only five feet two, but his ideals and his willingness to act them out were much bigger than his stature. Just possibly his sense of justice and responsibility derived from the unfairness of anti-Semitism he had to deal with in his youth in Russia.

I know little about Dad's history in Europe. Like many immigrants, he chose not to talk about the past. If only I had thought to ask him! He did tell me that his father was a manager, wine-taster and buyer for a landowner in Bessarabia, part of Russia on a border disputed with Romania. "In the mornings," Dad said, "I went down to the town square to see which flag was flying, and so which language I should speak that day!"

Interestingly wine seems to run in my family. My son was employed as a wine maker in California and my son-in-law is a home winemaker. I love to taste wine and I have a glass with my dinner every evening.

DEPRESSION 1930's

Fortunate to have work
standing forever
flat feet protected
on metal arches.

Immigrant cutting dresses
his bread and butter
his smile
barely cover his pain

Many tolls were taken
by the Collector
The Thirties.

ONLY THE DEAD*

To find work in the garment district
Does Dad still ride the Brooklyn local?
Read a stranger's discarded newspaper?
Others squeeze unseated in the express train.
When not hardscrabbling to feed his family
his inner life unexpressed
does he walk the Brooklyn streets alone,
cross the bridge to Manhattan
inexpensive solace
in the unemployed thirties?

Does he still smile at strangers
his unthreatening five-foot-two?

At home does he sleep away worries,
        flapdoor BVD's in summer,
        pajamas in winter?
Does he remain animated at family gatherings
where men play Pinochle
tease one another
drink a bit of schnapps
        to dull the edge of poverty?

Does dad know Brooklyn?
The dead know Brooklyn.

---

*From the title of the short story *Only the Dead Know Brooklyn* by Thomas Wolfe, 1935.

Another side to my father were his jokes, generally ironic:

In the early 1900's, a Jew was stopped by an officer of the czar's army, who demanded to know why Jews are so smart. After a moment the Jew replied, "Because we eat special herring." He took out a piece of herring from his pocket and began to eat it.

"Do you have any more of this special herring?" asks the officer.

The Jew replied, "A dozen pieces."

"What will you sell them for?" said the officer.

"Twenty rubles."

The officer paid, took a bite, and suddenly thought, "Wait a minute. In Moscow I could buy all this fish for a few kopecks."

"See," said the Jew, "You're getting smarter already."

Another of his jokes was more offensive, in fact repulsive, a reflection of the way Jews could express their fear and hostility toward the Nazis. For the overly sensitive, please close your eyes and ears.

In 1935 Hitler was prowling about the streets, looking for Jews. He caught a Jew and held a gun to his head. "Jew, you don't belong outside after hours. Pull down your pants! Now shit."

The Jew said, "But…"

"I said shit! Now eat it."

The Jew did what he was told, then rose quickly and grabbed the gun.

"Hitler, pull your pants down. Now shit, and it eat!"

"How dare you?" Hitler said.

" I said eat it," said the Jew, setting the trigger.

The Jew kept the gun on the Führer then rushed home. At home his wife asked, "How did you spend the day?"

Her husband replied, "I saw Hitler, and guess what? I had lunch with him."

Dad had funny expressions that were unique to him. "Eeenie-meenie- kotchka-dreenie." I have no idea where that came from, except as his response to "eenie-meenie-miniee-mo." Another was his explanation why people vary. "Some are different and others are different." Some of these linguistic oddities have carried over to me. I intentionally transform words: library becomes "libernary"; I call little carrots carrotskies; naphkishes for napkins; and a spoon is a shpoondel. My odd constructions had been influenced by the colorful Yiddish language I unfortunately never learned, other than several dozen words and phrases. The words sound Yiddish, but they arose from my abbreviated knowledge of the language that Mother discouraged me from learning. Escaping her childhood in Russia, she assimilated, only too completely. She wanted to Americanize me and wean me from her mother tongue. But overheard, some words of Yiddish got caught on my inner Velcro. The sounds and traces remain affectionately within me, especially in honor of Dad, who was comfortable using Yiddish, his native tongue.

THE FATHER IN THE SON

A supermarket a clerk picks up walnuts and crushes them together for me to sample. They are dry, sweet, ripe. I scoop a bunch of them into a plastic bag. At home I take two walnuts in my hand and try to crush them together.

I have a toothpick in my mouth that I carry along for hours.

Why do I do these things?

I remember that Dad often had a toothpick protruding from his mouth. And how strong I thought he was when he cracked open even a tough pair of walnuts in his closed fist. I try to do the same, but without success.

Years later I find myself unconsciously doing many things my father did. Our backgrounds, our histories are so different, his in Russia-Romania, mine in Brooklyn and California. He never owned a home or a car. He first had a telephone in his forties, while I was in college.

Unlike Dad, I had an excellent university education and advanced degrees. I never had to work to support the family during the Depression years. I own a house, a succession of cars and usual American gadgets. I own many acres of forestland. He died, one heart attack quickly following another at the age of 51. I am still going strong in my eighties. I undoubtedly inherited a genetic predisposition for heart disease. I required a quintuple bypass twenty years ago.

When Dad came home at the end of a day he changed to his pajamas, and in summer he stripped down to his BVD's and lay down to go *schlaffen*, sleep. A therapist once suggested to me that Dad's need for so much sleep might have been because he was depressed. Unlike Dad, I have high energy, cannot nap, and have been a poor sleeper since childhood. I used to think that sleep was waste of time, better spent in reading and doing.

Nevertheless, the toothpicks and walnuts exhibit that the father is in the son.

THE TROUBLE WITH HARRY

That was the title of a dark comedy film in 1955. In the movie, the trouble with Harry was that he died, and kept being buried over and over. Well, that isn't what this tale is about.

My father, Harry, had a well-to-do uncle also named Harry. Dad had just arrived with his mother and stepfather from Europe in 1919, a greenhorn in an Eastern European Jewish term, a recent immigrant who barely knew his way around this culture. Typically a greenhorn couldn't speak English, at least not "wery vell," emphasizing his greenness. Uncle Harry Charmoy was a relatively old settler, having come to America ten years before Dad.

As a dress-cutter, Dad worked for others on New York's

Fourth Avenue lineup of clothing factories. The elder Harry gave financial support to the younger Harry, that allowed him to go into the business of ladies dresses, facetiously called *schmattes*, i.e., rags in Yiddish. The business began to falter in 1929, the beginning of the Great Depression. Further, Dad fell prey to a dishonest partner, and the business was lost. From then on, my father remained a wage slave in the times of massive unemployment. For the most part he was out of work during the thirties, except for occasional seasonal work supplemented by selling wares on the streets of the city.

After Uncle Harry died, Dad had assumed he would inherit a small piece of his uncle's fortune. Alas, it would not be the first such disappointment for Dad. Uncle Harry didn't leave a will, and so all his money went to his widow, Aunt Adele. A few years later she married Mr. Simon, a man younger than she. Did he marry her for her money? Who knows? But my father remained out of luck. "*Sic transit gelt* (money)."

Dad accepted that the world was flawed, and while recognizing human frailty, he participated where he could. He was both supportive and skeptical of his trade union. A Socialist, as many poor Jewish immigrants were, he became an avid Roosevelt Democrat. He had strong convictions for economic and social justice, and he was one of the early members of the newly formed Liberal Party in New York State. Even with his limited resources, he contributed to anti-Nazi causes before and during World War II.

Women who knew him, including his many sisters-in-law, loved him. Even my mother, his constantly complaining wife, confessed to me that Dad was a truly loving, wonderful man, and she regretted that she complained to and about him so much.

My former wife, whose father was insensitive and downright cruel, found a new father in Dad. He liked women and treated them kindly and with respect. His relationship with men was also honest. Although he teased at times, it was with good-natured humor. He enjoyed verbal romps with his brothers-in-law during card games at family gatherings.

When his mother Sophie died, Dad thought he would inherit the house she owned. It was a modest old wooden house in the Jewish enclave of East New York in Brooklyn. Instead, the house went to her husband, Max Cooper, the grouchy house painter, whom she had married when her husband, my grandfather, died. Her husband inherited everything. There were no pre-nuptial agreements in those days, particularly for those who could not afford lawyers' fees.

However disappointed by these losses, my father took joy in his two sons. Although weary and worried financially, he kept it hidden from us, although we could read it in his drawn face. Only occasionally did he set his worry aside and became jaunty.

Eventually, life turned around when World War II was imminent. The Depression ended. Jobs were available, and Dad began to earn a steady income. His boys grew up, and photographs showed him relaxed, broadly smiling with my mother. For the first time in the years of their marriage they were untroubled by economic fears.

His smile, unfortunately, lasted only a few years after World War II ended. His and Mother's plans to visit my wife and me in California were snuffed out. A massive heart attack took Harry at age fifty-one. By then I was almost a father myself. Sadly, he never got to know his grandchildren who were cheated out of knowing him.

The trouble with Harry was that he left us too soon.

Mother and Dad in a happy time, a few years before his death.

SUMMERTIME AND THE LIVING IS EASY?

I wanted to have a job, though I had to convince my parents. Did they have too much pride to have their son work, were they concerned that I have free time in my childhood, or did my mother have a more selfish reason, that it would give me financial independence?

Eisenberg, a fat man with curly hair, owned a retail dairy. Dad hung out there, perhaps earning some money while working a limited amount for the owner. I got a job at the same dairy for a week, but their day started at five AM. I was relieved when my parents talked me out of continuing to work there.

I became a home delivery boy in the summer for the Brooklyn Daily Eagle. Purportedly it required only a few hours a day. During my first day I dodged unfriendly dogs, sweated profusely, and tried to match subscribers names with their addresses. By one PM I had barely finished, after finishing the route. Many of the customers lived in apartment houses, and that should have made it easier. However, the numbering of apartments varied from house to house, and I kept scouting for the right locations. It was a hot day, and I was exhausted when I arrived home. Mother decided that I should abandon the job, and I was all too willing to do so.

XI. STUYVESANT DAYS

I was thrilled, excited and a little overwhelmed. It was my first day at Stuyvesant High School. I was more proud than embarrassed to wear the school colors, a red and blue beanie. I received a booklet introducing the school, the extra-curricular activities, the words to the school songs, and everything one was supposed to know about his new school.

Stuyvesant specialized in the sciences. Entry was by examination, since the school was in great demand. I was allowed to enroll without examination as a sophomore, because of my ninth grade A record in junior high. At the time it was an all-boys school. Many years later Stuyvesant became co-ed. Entry by examination is still required.

The high school song "Old Peter Stuyvesant was a governor of New York, and a bold, brave and mighty man was he. And the wooden leg he walked upon as he trod the village green was the talk of the whole countree, was the talk of the whole countree." This was sung to the tune of "Old Jeffrey Amherst," the same tune that coincidentally my junior high school used for their song with appropriate lyrics.

Another song was, "Our strong band can ne'er be broken, formed in Stuyvesant High…" to the tune of Cornell's college song.

Having seen some other high schools, I was a bit surprised to see the building, shabby both inside and out. No athletic field, not even a blade of grass around the school. Other buildings surrounded the school on every side, including a woman's hospital. A Stuyvesant Campus did exist. It was a hot dog stand across the street that adopted the name.

Upperclassmen were quick to inform us freshies about the school. They told of the swimming pool on the sixth floor. The building had only five stories. We were supposed to take an elevator to get there. It was a hoax, and the elevator was off limits except for the staff and the handicapped. I doubt that many of us believed the hoaxers, because they were a bit too eager to tell us about the pool. But the story became an amusing tradition.

Notwithstanding the skimpy real estate and lack of a swimming pool, I relished reading and rereading the booklet that informed me that I was a Stuyvesantian, a proud mouthful. The naiveté of a newcomer to the school gave way in a short time to a blasé student. My teen-age mind could always find things to criticize.

Subsequently I learned that the original Peter Stuyvesant, for whom our high school was named, was a notorious anti-Semite who tried unsuccessfully to bar Jews from Manhattan. That took some of the polish off the brass.

Years later a new Stuyvesant was built on the West Side of Manhattan, overlooking the Hudson River. That school was an elegant, modern structure with accoutrements that were lacking in our old building, including television and music studios and at last a swimming pool.

Considering the lack of an athletic field, Stuyvesant managed to have track and football teams in my day. But to practice, one had to take a subway up to the Bronx, at least thirty minutes away. No wonder we won few games. Our high school did have a winning fencing team and a fair basketball team, both of which used our gym for practice. Unsurprisingly, we had champion chess and math teams, because of our academically selected students.

I joined the track team for a while, but the ride home from the Bronx to Brooklyn took over an hour. That was enough to end my running career in high school.

One of the first boys I met at Stuyvesant was a red-haired fellow whose mother had been divorced. It sounded racy! I was amazed by the notion of a divorce unconnected with Hollywood. The boy seemed a freak, but an interesting freak. Years later cousin Ella and Aunt Ada were divorced. That brought divorce closer to home. Nevertheless, years later when I was divorced I felt ashamed. But that is another story to be told another time.

One of my school friends, Alan P. had the privilege of running the mimeograph machine. That allowed him to do some extracurricular operations on it, like printing dirty jokes. I still have a copy of a "Peter Meter," that he ran off, commenting about the size of one's penis, a typical concern of males. "Eleven inches: Old Reliable—for exhibit purposes only." Seven inches is "For large women and small cattle." At the other end of the spectrum is: "One inch: just a water spout. You should have been a girl." More reasonable is "Five inches: The Woman's Home Companion." What did we know in those virginal early teens? But boys' and even men's fantasies were ever thus!

One of my favorites that Alan printed is, "What Type Are You?" describing the different ways that men urinate. Of the twenty on the list, a few especially stand out. "1. The frivolous man. He plays the stream up and down and across the urinal. Attempts to squirt flies. This type never grows up." Another is "14. The indifferent man. All urinals being occupied, he pees in the sink." Last on the list is: "20. The absent-minded man. He opens his vest, takes out his tie, then pisses in his pants." I often laugh out loud when I reread this historic list.

Traveling to the high school from Brooklyn was a memorable, if not attractive experience. Separate morning and afternoon sessions were necessary to serve its thousands of students. My first year was in the afternoon session. Morning session was reserved for the junior and senior years. To get to Manhattan I walked a half-mile to the local Culver elevated train station, paid the small fare, then rode to an express stop and switched to either the West End or Sea Beach Line. I got off at Fourteenth Street, Union Square, and walked another half mile to the school on Fifteenth Street and Second Avenue. The whole trip took an hour each way.

The elevated train on the Culver Line was relatively empty after early rush hour. Because the station was unattended at the hour, I had to insert a nickel in a slot and a rotating metal door from near the floor almost to the ceiling allowed access to the station. Even though the fare was cheap, some boys loved to beat the system. There were two ways to do this. I observed one in which a boy climbs on another's shoulders and both enter for a single fare. The second way may be apocryphal. Supposedly a boy would urinate into the coin slot and enter free. Urine is an electrical conductor. Human ingenuity knows no bounds. Of course salt water would do an even better job, if the premise was true, but urine makes a much better story.

Often I met Wally and Feinstein whom we called "Fink" when I changed to the West End Line. I don't think I ever knew Feinstein's first name. We teased one another, but the butt was primarily Fink. He was a smiling, good-natured fellow who wore a porkpie hat. He beat out dance steps while humming songs. In the terminology of the time he was a hepcat. All I remember about Wally is his heavy sweater bearing a band name and clef. I haven't been able to trace them using alumni records.

If I arrived early, I stopped at Union Square on my walk across town to school. Men on figurative and actual soapboxes gave their spiels. Some were holy Joes, offering eternal life. Others were political haranguers. One regular radical spouted anti-capitalist talk. The magazines *Time, Life and Fortune* became "Crime, Strife, and Misfortune." The *New York Daily News* and The *Herald Tribune* were transformed to The Daily Noise and The Herald Spittoon.

A girls' high school, Washington Irving, was nearby, and occasionally there were girls on the Square. One time I saw friend and classmate Joshua Lederberg earnestly trying to coach a girl in her mathematics homework. She looked moon-eyed at him, perhaps grasping the subject, but mostly taking in his male presence. While oblivious to her wiles, he continued to teach her. He referred to himself as the Last Puritan at the time. As the years went by and he entered college, he gave up that self-characterization and joined the rest of us males with our desires.

In 1958, Josh was awarded a Nobel Prize in biology. I visited Stuyvesant many years later, hoping to be recognized as a conquering hero. But when I mentioned my class of 1941, the reaction invariably was, "That was the year Joshua Lederberg graduated." Crestfallen, I left with a wan smile. Sadly as I write this, I learned that Josh has died recently. We had been old friends in high school and college. We had him over for dinner in my high school days. But that was before his fame as a Nobel Laureate, and he seemed to have forgotten me.

Returning home on the subway wasn't a leisurely trip. People returning from work were sandwiched into the crowded trains. The high point for me was crossing the Williamsburg Bridge when the subway emerged from the dark underground. I could see the docks in Brooklyn and inhale fresh coffee from the roasters. Many years later the same scent followed me when I crossed the Bay Bridge to San Francisco. I guess coffee was roasted at the place where the beans arrived from abroad.

A junior the next year, I was in the morning session that started at eight o'clock. I transferred to an express train that was packed with wage and salaried slaves. Togetherness had a special meaning in the early morning, with body pressed against body. Women held their purses in front of them to protect their breasts. There was little they could do to protect their backsides. Some people tried to read newspapers in the cattle-car, and their papers sometimes brushed against my nose. I had a lesson in what to me was odd behavior once when I felt a hand grasping my genitals. Surprised at first, I quickly exited at the next subway stop and entered another train. It certainly gave me a queer feeling, and that was before we used the word in its current sense. I never did see the guilty one, nor did I care to.

To depart at Fourteenth Street, I had to worm my way to the sliding door before the doors closed. Most of the passengers worked farther uptown and remained in the car.

After the morning classes, I sat high in the auditorium on a seat with its rounded wooden back, polished by years of sitting students. I would nibble the sandwich Mother had packed for me. Like other self-absorbed teenagers, I doubt that I appreciated her preparation. I felt it was my due.

While I ate my cream cheese and jelly sandwich and sipped milk, showers of music sprinkled over me from the senior orchestra in rehearsal. I enjoyed the music and envied the players. Mozart's thirty-ninth Symphony remains embedded in my musical memory. In my imagination I am back in the auditorium. I hear the deep rumbling resonance of Ben Lepson's bassoon, and I recall his lisp. Probably his family was more well-to-do than mine. Why else would he be playing a bassoon instead of a violin? Indeed, he later enrolled in $ Harvard $.

After school I often strolled down Fourth Avenue investigating the many bookstores that sold used books. What a feast! After spending only few nickels, I boarded the almost empty train for my return home. The few inexpensive book treasures I had bought expanded my limited library.

On a visit to the city fifteen years ago I felt sad that the bookstores were all gone, transformed to coffee houses, boutiques, and other establishments that could pay higher rents. Ghosts of the many small bookshops, however, still haunted Fourth Avenue for me.

One Friday afternoon, as the herd of students cattled their way down the stairs to go home, I jumped up joyously on the bottom step and came down in a pool of blood. I had hit my head on the cement riser above. I spent the next few hours in the women's hospital nearby. When I arrived home a few hours later with a massive bandage on my head, Mother was aghast. Unsuccessfully I tried to calm her. "It's OK, Mom, its not serious."

Years later my hairline climbed above my forehead, and the remnants of a scar from the injury was exposed.

In my senior year, I traveled homeward with my friend Dick, who lived a few blocks from me. An attractive brunette, a few years older than we were was in the subway car. We decided to follow her, fantasizing that she might be interested in us. We took the train past our normal stop and she got out. Then we returned to our station. Nothing ventured, nothing gained, though we didn't even speak to her. Blame it on our testosterone and our high school that had no girls at the time.

HIGH SCHOOL TEACHERS

Most of our teachers were very good. There were a few notable exceptions. I remember my chemistry teacher, just short of five feet tall, in his khaki lab coat full of acid-produced holes. He gave us mimeograph sheets to copy, to COPY! into our notebook, later to be examined by him. This was memorization, not science. He reminded me of Christopher Robin's Eeyore the way he droned dolefully, "A lot of you guys are gonna flunk." He remains nameless, as Mr. L. This kind of teaching without zest in any science class was outrageous and never should have been tolerated. But teachers were autonomous.

Mr. Schwartz taught history. With his full moustache and wild hair, he looked like a pudgy Groucho Marx, and had a similar insulting humor. When a boy raised his hand to go to what is euphemistically referred to as the bathroom, he would say, "Sit down. Hold your water. I'll give you a rubber band."

Our bow-tied economics teacher, Mr. Zuckerman was an energetic man, moved quickly, and was an excellent teacher, almost dancing as he lectured. As I write this, more than sixty years later, I have just read his obituary in our alumni news. He died at ninety-five.

My Latin teachers were Miss Lewin and Mr. Schabacker.

Mr. Schabacker was a balding man in his fifties, with a droning voice and a dry manner. He told us that when he studied Latin, his teacher made the same joke every year at a particular passage. And so the students wrote in their textbook at this passage, *locus ioci*, that translates as "place of a joke."

Miss Lewin looked the part of what used to be called an old maid or more kindly, a maiden lady, with brown horn-rim glasses. From my perspective as a teen, I assumed she was thirty or forty. A pleasant, agreeable woman with a plain, but not unattractive face, she was a good teacher. But what attracted my attention, impelled by my testosterone-driven body, were her shapely legs that her transparent stockings revealed. I felt like a lascivious character. Later I was relieved to learn that my friend Ubert also admitted that he stared at her legs.

Ubert, a light-skinned African American lived in Harlem. We were close at school, but we were separated by too many subway stops and sadly, the racial barrier. He had his friends and I had mine.

Years later I located Miss Lewin through the phone book and arranged to visit her. I really liked her (not only for her legs!) We talked about Latin, my career, and her current life. She had never married. We had a rewarding visit, and she expressed gratitude that I had thought enough to meet her. Of course I never mentioned the bit about her legs!

A history teacher, Mr. D., with his shock of white hair, tyrannized us. He would ask a question, then look down through his reading glasses, and search the names in his grading book. A silence followed that seemed endless. Who would be the unlucky one selected? Looking over the top of his glasses, he called the victim's name. The boy usually felt intimidated, and invariably answer incorrectly or not at all. The teacher made a mark, presumably a black one, in the Book of the Damned. He would then scan the names further, and after a pregnant pause

146

to heighten the drama, select another victim. I dreaded going to his class. I suspect the teacher probably tore wings off flies in his free time. At night before bed, I prayed in my atheistic way that he would die and save me from his tortures.

One day not long after my prayers I felt shocked, relieved, and guilty when a substitute teacher told us he had died of a heart attack the previous night. In assembly his death was announced. As usual when a teacher died, we sang, "Abide With Me."

Could I have actually brought on his death? My rational mind said no, but it was frightening to think I might have a power to kill just by wishing.

On the other hand, there were other teachers who were really inspiring. Mr. Simon was an excellent physics instructor. Solomon Greenfield was a delightful trigonometry teacher and punster. He presented the riddle: "Why is an inclined plane like a lazy dog?" The answer, "Because it is a slow pup (slope-up)."

Some of our English teachers had other pursuits. Joseph Shipley edited *The Dictionary of World Literature*. I bought a copy many years after I graduated and it remains on my bookshelf. He was also a theater critic.

Mr. Mostow, who taught the senior English class acted as scholarship advisor. When I told him that I would be majoring in chemical engineering, he immediately responded, "Oh no!" Perhaps Mostow knew more about me than I had admitted to myself, that I didn't seem the engineering type. Perhaps he recognized the inchoate writer and poet in me that I wasn't in touch with, that didn't emerge from the undergrowth until many years later. In his English class I had written essays and short stories, and he sensed my love of words. But I doggedly pursued chemical engineering. I liked pure chemistry, and found that I didn't like most of my engineering courses, except for one taught by a physical chemist, Phil Schutz. I liked him and in his reserved but smiling way, he liked me. Years afterward I would have met him in my graduate school days at UC Berkeley. I was saddened and shocked to hear that he died of cancer just before he was to be on the Berkeley faculty.

In those Depression years a steady job was what mattered, especially for the son of poor immigrants. Mother's brothers, educated and employed as engineers also had an influence in my choice. Years after my retirement from a technical career, the writing Muse came scratching on my window pane. I let her in happily, and began to write prose and poetry that has continued.

Mr. Mostow, scholar, teacher, and accessible man of quiet dignity died prematurely a few years after I graduated from Stuyvesant.

I wish I could remember the name of one of my English teachers, a young man who read poetry to us with such sensitivity. To this day I can almost hear his sensuous reading of "The Raven," "Annabel Lee," and "El Dorado." It was my first appreciation of poetry. Maybe that's why after a long career in science and engineering, quite barren of poetry, I began to write poems. Some of them have been published and won awards.

By contrast with the nameless teacher, I remember a boring history teacher, Mr. M, who droned on without conveying any excitement about the past. I had to write a paper each week about some aspect of history. I remained uninterested in history until I watched some documentary programs on public television.

Substitute teachers often had a challenging experience when they took over a class, even a normally well-behaved group of students, who often give them a lot of guff. Sometimes the teachers inadvertently ask for it. We had an attractive substitute teacher, a woman with reddish-blonde hair. Some students named her the Simonized blonde, since it appeared that her hair had an assist from the bottle. She began the class by writing her name on the blackboard. I doubt whether we would have addressed her by other than that name, but she announced that she was "Mrs. Axelrod, NOT Axlegrease." The class promptly responded in unison, "Yes, Mrs. Axlegrease!"

WQXR

As I listen today to the strains of Tchaikovsky's waltz from his opera *Eugene Onegin,* I drift back to my youth and WQXR, a music station in New York City. I listened to all the warhorses. Today they return me to that not quite forgotten time, probably better in the recollection than the reality. But the past is like that for most (all?) of us.

It was early morning on a school day, and I arose to get ready for the day. Mother had already prepared breakfast and packed a lunch for me. The music was for her pleasure as well as a delightful way to keep me awake. A singing advertisement for Wrigley's Spearmint gum, was interspersed with the music for this was and still is a commercial music station. The commercials seemed annoying at the time, but like many things from the past, it remains a fond memory. The words and music still ring in my ears.

WQXR accompanied me during the afternoon when I returned from school, and on Saturday, following a shower after a handball game. The station followed me to college, and I continued to listen to the station until I left New York. Another remembrance was the advertisement of Gambarelli and Davito, touting their wines.

WQXR is a real survivor, still playing music today.

DEVELOPING INTEREST IN SCIENCE.

While in high school I continued to follow my early interest in science, especially chemistry. I mentioned laboratory experiments with my friend Norman, and my fascination with mineralogy, that came to an unfortunate end, though not from a lack of interest. At twelve years of age, I had bought an examination review book for high school chemistry and devoured it. Before I took a required chemistry class in high school three years later, I would have easily been able to pass a final exam in the subject. Another reflection of an interest in science was my subscription to Popular Science. The magazine was more concerned with new technology than science per se, but I was intrigued with new inventions and where technology would point to in the future. I read the magazine from cover to cover and used it as a basis for some essays in high school. Later in life I lost my interest in technology as contrasted to pure science.

RUINED(?) BY READING

A contest a few years ago had the facetious title "Ruined by Reading." In a sense I was "ruined" by reading. I learned to read at age four. Although I didn't read Shakespeare then, I did read children's books. I progressed to *Alice in Wonderland.* Alice was pictured in color on the cover of a book, a tattered, old gift that I still own. She looks at the white rabbit hurrying away, his watch in hand. The delightful sketches in the book include my favorite, the Cheshire cat.

Tom Sawyer followed, another book I still own, its binding almost in shreds. The cover picture depicts a classic scene in which Tom tricks boys to whitewash the fence, their payment for the privilege of releasing him from his task, while he happily chews on an apple.

The front page of both these books attests to my quavering signature at age eight.

Uncle Abe gave me a gift of *Alice in Orchestralia,* by Ernest LaPrad, a takeoff of the original Alice book, in which musical instruments tell about their roles in the orchestra. I no longer own the book, although recently I relived the pleasure of reading it from a copy loaned from a distant library.

As I grew older, I began to read the Hardy Boys and their adventures. *Hunting for Hidden Gold,* was one of a hundred books of the series. In high school I was introduced to Poe. I indulged in *Murders in the Rue Morgue*. I learned about Louis

Pasteur, Paul Ehrlich, and other medical discoverers in Paul de Kruif's *Microbe Hunters.*

During summer vacations I devoured many novels. I recall the best seller, Pietro di Donato's *Christ in Concrete.* At sixteen I was impressed by its intensity. The protagonist inadvertently became entombed in cement poured while he labored in the construction of a building. The book especially captivated me because I watched several apartment buildings being built on my street.

I read many more books, but most of their titles remain unnumbered and unremembered. A najor "ruination" came when the *New York Post* offered a twenty-volume set of Dickens with a subscription to the newspaper. We had little money, but at twenty-five cents a week, the total cost was only five dollars, spread over months. The low-cost option we bought was bound in brown. The more expensive version, thirty-five cents weekly, had blue bindings. After completing my high school homework in the evening, I had about thirty minutes before my eyes began to close, and so I read fifteen or twenty pages. The next night I had to back up a page to get the drift, and so it took many evenings to go through the whole book. *Pickwick Papers,* a volume of more than 700 pages consumed many weeks.

I squeezed in other Dickens books during the school year, *A Tale of Two Cities, Little Dorrit,* and *David Copperfield.* Mother sent me the set after many years. I retain only four of the original volumes, including that of Mr. Pickwick.

When I discovered Sherlock Holmes, I gorged on his adventures and the amazing, if somewhat unbelievable deductions of the master.

One summer afternoon I began to read Steinbeck's *Grapes of Wrath.* I continued through the night, my eyes devouring the words. The last few pages moved me to tears. Rose o' Sharon who had just lost her baby, nursed a dying old man with her milk. Notwithstanding some crotchety critics (sometimes I think they are mostly crotchety) I have always considered Steinbeck one of America's greatest authors because of his character portrayals and his genuine humanity, and of course the literary quality of his writings. Many years later I was Tom Joad. I composed my lines for a reenacted performance of a part of the book.

What do I mean by ruined by reading? I became so enamored of books that I can't resist buying them far in excess of what I can possibly read. My bookcases overflow throughout my house, and I continue to buy more books. A dozen books, some currently from the public library, are piled or scattered on the floor next to my bed. I support and champion public libraries. I frequent our local library several times a week. The librarians and I are on a first name basis. Nevertheless, I still buy books. It is almost an obsession, if not an addiction. I barely look at television, even the so-called good programs. Book mania is mine.

If this is ruin, I don't regret it. In case I haven't made it obvious, I love books. Perhaps a more appropriate title would be "Ruined by Books."

XII. EIGHTEENTH AVENUE

Dad had been working when he could, but the Depression continued, and work was seasonal. As a dress cutter, a typical job for an immigrant Eastern European Jew, he was an employee. Sales were as bleak as a February day in Brooklyn, and more often than not, Dad was out of work.

He proposed that we buy a retail bakery. The goods would be delivered from actual bakeries. Mother and Dad scouted a likely place to see how many customers could be expected. Satisfied that they would be able to eke out a living, they bought a business on Eighteenth Avenue in Brooklyn. We moved a half-mile from our apartment on Ocean Parkway.

Dad rose at dawn, bringing in the bakery items, milk, and other commodities. Across the avenue was an elementary school. Mother prepared luncheons for the teachers to add to our income. She also rose early and began to cook in order to be ready for the onslaught. At noon the teachers swooped in, chatting continuously, in a hurry to be fed. They were a privileged lot at the time having regular jobs when others were unemployed. Some teachers complained, expecting immediate service, even though a horde of them came in at the same time. Mother felt that many of them were arrogant and ungrateful for her efforts. Most took Mother's tasty lunches for granted, although occasionally a considerate person would compliment her for the quality of the lunch. Meals were less than a dollar, leaving little for profit.

Business was slow. Money was scarce in 1939. Small retailers couldn't compete with A&P chain store prices. Our customers often bought only a bottle of milk and a few rolls. Mother, who had been ambivalent about having the store, began to complain. In the past, she had to take care of the household while Dad went off to work or looked for work. Now she had to help keep the store and cook meals for the teachers, in addition to keeping house, washing, ironing, and preparing the family meals.

My parents slept in a small room in the back of the store. Upstairs, my brother Eddy and I shared a double bed in a small bedroom. I commuted by subway to high school in Manhattan, an hour's trip from door to door. I often thought with regret that if I had gone to Erasmus Hall, the local co-ed high school, I would have walked the mile with boys and girls. At age nine, my brother merely walked across Eighteenth Avenue to school.

For the short time we lived on the avenue, I had new friends who knew one another, but I was able to shoehorn my way in. Steve, whose warm smile exposed braces on his teeth, had a serious relationship with a quiet, pretty girl. They were only fifteen, but planned to get married, presumably in the distant future. I wonder if they did.

Jerry, a guy even shorter than I, was a good mimic. He imitated Bob Hope's Jerry Colonna, who remarked when coming on the scene, "Greetings Gate, let's inebriate," or another rhyming word. Jerry turned it around teenwise and said, "Greetings Gate, lets masturbate." He fancied himself a singer, as well as a mimic. He crooned current popular songs. The one I remember was, "Little girl, you're the one girl for me…"

We boys went to a matinee at a local movie house. Some kids sneaked in through the exit door. The theater may have been well taken care of in the earlier heyday of films, but now run down, it had threadbare seats and peeling paint. We called it The Itch. Years later, the writer Pete Hamill referred to a theater that was similarly named. Could it have been the same theater? He was, after all, from Brooklyn.

In the manner of teenage boys, we annoyed the adults in the movie house by hooting and shouting until the manager tried to stop us and finally booted us out.

SHOWER PLEASURE

The time is now; the time is then. Both interweave as I feel the spray of a shower, cleansing and warming my skin. I have just returned from a vigorous hike to renew my frequent communion with Ma Nature. As I luxuriate in the sudsy warmth, I return to then.

Then was at age fifteen on Eighteenth Avenue. As a teenager I lived in my own world, barely oblivious to that of my parents who were trying to run the store. My world was commuting to high school. Plenty of homework, and I was a conscientious student.

But Saturdays were different. Then handball in a nearby schoolyard was king. I occasionally won a game, but those times were infrequent. One day I played against Dougherty, an amiable Irish-American boy. He usually beat me, but I always tried again. Gangly and much taller than me, he swung close to the ground to make a killer. The ball hit the wall so low that it rolled back instead of bouncing so I couldn't return it. He won again. I waited my turn to challenge the next game's winner, maybe to suffer another loss.

The afternoon waned. I went indoors to the shower where the water's warmth healed my losses. I felt refreshed and happy to be alive, an infrequent feeling in my adolescence. To add to my contentment, WQXR, the New York City classical music station was playing the usual war-horses that I had become used to. The late afternoon sun stole through a curtain-covered window, a silent obbligato to my contented mood. There would be other days, other games. I will win a few, but the warm shower's aftermath and music on the radio would always be there to comfort me as it did that day.

Thinking about the past, I heave a reminiscent sigh and luxuriate in the long shower as I did then.

Scientist at Work. Science Competition

SCIENCE COMPETITION

In my senior year at Stuyvesant I enrolled in an optional post-grad class, called Physics Lab, where we did research of our own choosing. The project I chose was the chemistry of colloids. I was attracted to colloids because of the unusual behavior and colors of the chemicals. I suspect my love of chemistry was as much aesthetic as scientific.

I had my own laboratory in the dark basement of the store. I did many of my experiments there that continued the ones I did at school, in preparation for the upcoming science fair. After finishing my assigned homework at night I retreated to the basement. I did my research on a work table lit by one bare light bulb dangling from above. I felt discomfited by the intermittent scrambling sounds of rats in the dark corners of the cellar. For weeks I performed my work, continuing each night until Mother called down for the third time, "Albert, come upstairs to bed. It's late and tomorrow is school."

Those same rats, or perhaps their cousins, appeared at compromising times in the store. While waiting on a customer, my parents saw a large rat in a corner behind the counter that they didn't want the shopper to see. Keeping cool heads, they served the person, then broomed the rat away after the door closed behind the unknowing customer.

Mother's vocal complaints became stronger about the demanding nature of her work, the long hours, and the rats. Dad agreed to sell the business. I was intrigued by how they went about this. When potential buyers were to arrive, all our friends and relatives were asked to visit the store as supposed customers to make it appear that business was booming. It was an old New York trick, and probably had been used on us when we purchased this store. Finally, we sold the business. We moved to an apartment on Ocean Parkway once more, and I lost my laboratory.

My time in the basement had not been wasted. I prepared

an outline of my talk for the upcoming science fair. I collected my chemicals and apparatus. Saturday morning arrived for the city-wide Science Fair competition. A number of high school boys and girls gathered at the American Museum of Natural History in Manhattan. I constantly reviewed mentally what I would present, and kept revising my outline.

At 10:30 it was my turn. My first words were shaky. As I got more deeply into my talk, I began to relax and talked more easily. One of the experiments went slightly awry, but I improvised and fixed it.

In thirty minutes I completed my presentation, after I hurriedly rushed the last few minutes to keep within my time limit. The small audience applauded. I responded with an embarrassed grin, and took a deep breath.

I was impressed with the competing projects, most of them constructions rather than lecture-demonstrations like mine, and so I had little expectation of winning.

Several hours later the judges announced the winners. I was surprised and pleased that I had been awarded first prize— a medal and an overnight train trip to visit the Westinghouse Research Labs near Pittsburgh, Pennsylvania.

Two weeks later I boarded the sleeper at Penn Station in New York. Actually "sleeper" is a misnomer. My excitement, the clicking of the wheels, the unsteady rocking of the train, and the heat in the upper berth conspired to keep me awake most of the night. It was my first overnight railroad trip and my first trip away from home.

In the morning I was greeted at the station by Floyd, a Westinghouse employee. He drove me to the company's location in nearby Wilkinsburg. A photographer took my picture for newspaper stories in New York and Pittsburgh. Floyd gave me a guided tour of their laboratories, and afterwards took me to dinner with several Westinghouse researchers.

Afterward I was taken to a Benny Goodman concert. I was surprised to see that his singer, Peggy Lee, appeared not much older than I. She looked small and vulnerable. Her voice, appealing for its almost little girl quality, had not fully matured.

That night I slept well at a nearby hotel. After a day touring the manufacturing facility, and another night in the hotel, I returned home on the train.

I was pleased to see my picture and the article about me in the newspaper. I was also invited to be a demonstrator at the Westinghouse exhibit in the 1939 New York World's Fair.

I had a number of mementos and memories of the trip. Peggy Lee became one of my favorite popular singers, and I felt almost proprietary about Benny Goodman's band. An unusual memory that soon faded was the soot on my shirt collar and handkerchiefs. Pittsburgh had not yet cleaned up its air.

Peggy's singing had a haunting quality and she seemed almost distant, while being present at the same time, as though she were singing from a hidden corner of the room. I have enjoyed her songs on recordings, some of which she had composed. I read that in later years she had a stroke and that she came on stage using a walker and in a tent-like structure because of her difficulty in breathing, another victim of the tobacco menace.

I learned with sadness that Miss Peggy, as she was known, had died at the age of 81. For me she will always be the eighteen year-old singer with an even younger voice.

But for now—
Goodbye, Eighteenth Avenue
Goodbye, Bakery
Goodbye, Rats
Farewell, Pittsburgh.

THE WORLD'S FAIR AND THE IRON MAN

My primary hero is Harry Rothman, my father. My other heroes are an odd assortment—Albert Einstein, Wolfgang Mozart, John Steinbeck, George Gershwin, and Lou Gehrig, Probably others who don't come to mind. Imagine an opportunity to meet and be with one of them!

Most of my friends were Dodger fans, although there was a scattering of those who rooted for the Giants. I was an ardent Yankee fan because of Babe Ruth, Red Ruffing, Hank Crosetti, among others, but especially Lou Gehrig.

As the Science winner of a competition, I had an invitation to be an exhibitor, molding plastics for Westinghouse at the New York Worlds Fair in 1939. I received a free two-week pass to visit all the other exhibits and buildings with the badge I was given.

I entered the new blue train to Flushing Meadows, the site of the fairground and the emblems of the fair, the Trylon tower and Perisphere, a giant sphere depicting the world. I enjoyed wandering about, going on various rides, and seeing the exhibits. Among them was General Motor's Futurama, a diorama of a supposedly wonderful future, seen from a chair on a moving conveyor. Even Hitler's Germany and Mussolini's Italy had buildings and exhibitions, since our entry in WW II was still in the future. I chose to avoid their propaganda.

I drifted around, listening to the hawkers selling their gimmicks. One in particular captured my attention. He was selling a circular kazoo-like aluminum item that one could hum or sing with. The hawker entertained the crowd with many songs played on his kazoo. After awhile he chased me away to leave more space for others. That reminded me of a movie with W. C. Field talking out of the side of his mouth, "Get along, Sonny!" I felt like that kid, and slipped back to the middle of the crowd to keep listening to the showman. Years later I heard that Gregory Peck had also been a hawker at the fair. With all my meanderings there, I may well have passed him, of course without knowing about his future fame.

I drank the buzzy sweetness Coca Cola for the first time and lunched on mustard-smothered hot dogs. But best of all, I attended a baseball school with Lou Gehrig.

Lou was just as warm, personable, and kind as his reputation. He spoke with authority and yet softly. He patiently showed us how to hold the bat and swing for power. Lou looked like the powerhouse he was—muscular build and sturdy legs. In person, his famous smile, dimples showing, was even more inviting than in photographs. The class lasted only an hour, and though it was so many years ago, I recall that hour clearly. I still have the card addressed to me and signed by Gehrig that certified my attendance.

Lou first played baseball at Columbia University. Years later he came down with the disease that was named after him, much easier to say than Amyotropic Lateral Sclerosis, but just as devastating. The Iron Man became so weak that he had to quit baseball. The crowd cheered at his last appearance in Yankee Stadium, when he uttered those often-repeated words, "I'm the luckiest man alive." Not long afterwards, the great ballplayer died. The nation mourned him, as I did. I had been so fortunate to meet him in person, and even shake his hand.

Later I lost interest in the Yankees because they always seemed to win. Then I reclaimed my origins and began to root for the underdogs, the Brooklyn Dodgers.

Most boys at the time seemed to know all the players, their batting averages and other statistics. In my attempt to gain the acceptance of my peers, I tried to memorize that information. Frustrated and bored, I gave up and lost all interest in professional teams. I don't understand fan loyalties, since teams often change their geographical connections. Unlike many men and women, I am not a sports fan.

In 1939 I took a baseball class from one of my heroes, Lou Gehrig.

Eventually the Dodgers abandoned Brooklyn for Los Angeles, and I abandoned the East for the West Coast for entirely different reasons, to be taken up in a later memoir.

FIELD TRIPS

In my junior year, our high school sponsored a local trip to Bellevue, a vast, city-funded hospital. After we were escorted through the place, I was left with two vivid and related memories. One was the morgue. The other was the intrusive smell of formaldehyde that permeated the hospital. If I ever had a predilection to become a physician, the formaldehyde would have convinced me not to. The visit made me associate the smell with hospitals and death.

We had another trip to Polytechnic Institute, a technical college in Brooklyn, much later to be named Polytechnic University. I remember standing on the fire escape on the eighth floor. Through the metal grating on the floor, I looked down to the ground level. It was a frightening view, and I felt a strange, powerful pull to jump over the edge. I held on to the protective bar in fear of this irrational attraction. A few years later while working in Connecticut I commuted to night classes at Poly and received a Master's degree—another time in a memoir to come.

HIGH SCHOOL GRADUATION

It was graduation time for the Class of January 1941. Our autograph books had been signed by friends and a few teachers. Because space in our school was so limited, graduation ceremonies were held in Carnegie Hall. I think of the musician's joke, "How do you get to Carnegie Hall? Practice, practice, practice." For us the practice was four years of high school.

High School Grad, 1941

I sat with my parents waiting for the ceremony. After a Mendelssohn March and the National Anthem, Jean Cook, an African-American boy orated his composition, "Democracy on Trial." The Gypsy Baron Overture followed, and an oration by Elmer Hurt, another student. Then the First Movement of Mozart's G-Minor Symphony, one of my favorites. Harry S. Rogers, President of Polytechnic Institute of Brooklyn gave the customary address to the graduates. More music, then the presentation of prizes by Dr. Shipley, an English teacher. Suddenly I heard my name called. I stepped forward to receive an award in chemistry, then one for Latin, one for physics, another for classics, and finally one for general scholarship. I graduated second in my class of 500. Frank Clark was first, and Jean Cook, third. I have exchanged mail with Jean who moved to Paris later in life, but I have no idea what happened to Frank. More music by the high school orchestra and then the awarding of diplomas by Principal Sinclair Wilson, followed by the school song "Our Strong Band Can Ne'er Be Broken," sung to the same tune coincidentally as that of Germany's anthem *"Deutschland Uber Alles."* Finally, the Mendelssohn recessional and the event was over.

Parenthetically, I have been in touch with Jean Cook who recently passed away.

Occasionally I took the train to 23rd Street in Manhattan from my home in Brooklyn. With money I was able to cadge from Mother, I bought a few chemicals and some laboratory glassware at J. H. Winn's store. In addition to their utility, I loved the shapes of Erlenmeyer and Florence flasks. With those purchases I developed a minilab of my own.

THE BIG STINK

Although I graduated from high school in January 1941, I decided to stay on at Stuyvesant since college classes didn't begin until September. I took Qualitative Analysis, an advanced chemistry class. Each of us was given a different, so-called unknown solution and we were to determine what was in the liquid. The solution had to be treated with hydrogen sulfide gas to precipitate metal sulfides. The color of the precipitate determined the metal in question. Various treatments were required to determine the other components. I fell ill, unable to complete the tests in school, and so I brought my unknown sample home. Using my laboratory equipment and chemicals, I generated hydrogen sulfide, a foul gas that smells like rotten eggs. Inhalation in significant quantities is poisonous, although the stink is so bad, one can easily avoid toxic levels. On a cold winter's day I placed the experiment on a window-sill when my mother's attention was elsewhere. Eventually I did finish the analysis. I don't remember whether I got it right or not. Because of the cold weather, yellow, orange, and red polysulfides were formed. These were the same colloids that had fascinated me in my junior year and helped me to win the prize at the Science Fair. I became even more interested in these complex compounds.

XIII. SOME DIVERSIONS

Ones that didn't easily fit in above.

NEW YORK SUBWAY

I didn't fully appreciate the subways until I left New York. One could travel all over the city for many hours and miles. In my youth the cost was a mere five cents. Much later the fare was over a dollar, and tokens were sold at the entrance. Even above a dollar, the cost was a token pittance, pun unintended, still cheap by current standards. Bus connections were easy and frequent. For comparison I think of the difficulty of trying to get to many parts of San Francisco even with our rapid transit BART. One requires many transfers and separate fares to bus lines. Even worse was travel to the rest of the Bay Area, either with or without an automobile.

I'm now a Californian, an outdoors person. Living in New York would feel too confining, although I occasionally lapse into sentimentality about my past life in the city. However, I do yearn for the ease of traveling by public transportation.

ROOFTOPS

Mother experienced the horror of the rooftops in Kiev, where ignorant, bigoted Russians persecuted Jews. ("If you prick us, do we not bleed?" W. Shakespeare.)

Easter was a hated holiday among Jews, when the priests stirred up the ignorant masses and the violent ones to avenge the killing of a Jew 2000 years ago by killing innocent Jews later. After Easter services, the Cossacks sought out Jews all over Russia and Poland. In Kiev, where Mother's family lived, the Cossacks would arrive at an apartment house and ask, "Any

Jews here?" Most of the gentile neighbors would deny that any were there. But a few would say "no," and wink, tipping off the aggressors. The soldiers then climbed the stairs to search and destroy. Mother's family and other Jews would climb to the rooftops, and walk or jump to adjacent rooftops to escape. It was like another underground railway that slaves in America used to escape, only this time it was well above ground.

The rooftop played a more positive role in my life. It enriched my life in apartment houses in Brooklyn. Open space seemed born into my genes. The city was too enclosed for me, even in Brooklyn where there were no Manhattan-like skyscrapers. Although not a conscious thought then, the artificiality of a rather man-made (man-mad?) environment stifled me. So on rain-free days I brought my homework and pleasure reading to the roof in daylight hours. My environment became the sky and clouds, a vast open space. Much later I understood the significance of my escape to the roof, when my deep passion for open space and wilderness emerged.

Pigeon coops were wire structures kept on the roofs. A hobby was flying homing pigeons. My cousin-in-law Dick loved creatures. He trained pigeons to fly home, from increasing distances. Later he raced them in competitions. They were carried in cages at least fifty miles away and released. The first birds to return to their home bases were declared the winners.

THE RUSSIAN DENTIST

I sit in a modern dentist's office in Livermore, California surrounded by the latest stainless steel accoutrements. Helen, the dental hygienist, is cleaning my teeth. I lie back in the chair, bored by the so-called light rock music. It is sloughing out of the speaker system into the treatment rooms and originates from a local radio station.

As I stare into the examination light, my mind wanders to another time. I was a high school student in New York, sitting in a dentist's office on a torn, aging brown leather chair. The overhead dental tools had a dull metallic finish. They were old-fashioned even for the time. Unlike the lightness of today's office, the room was dark and the walls smoke-dimmed in the windowless room. Bits of peeling paint hung from the ceiling. On one of the walls was a photograph of a handsome young officer astride a horse, sword by his side.

The dentist, Sergei, was a Russian emigré, who left after the Russian revolution. He said to me, "I vas vonce a cavalryman in the Czar's army." Aha! The photograph. He had traded one uniform for another. Now he wore a short white dental gown, below which peered dark brown trousers that shone from wear. His tie was akimbo, and a more than adequate belly seemed to belie a military silhouette. He did, however, punctuate his sentences with an occasional click of his heels. His was a one-man effort, without a dental hygienist. As he leaned over me, I smelled the heavy scent of stale tobacco, especially when he cleared his throat, as he did frequently. I saw space between his head and a dark toupee, the first I had ever observed up close.

His English was barely adequate. I asked him to repeat his words, while pretending that I understood him. I was too embarrassed to ask him to repeat more than once. The candy I used to assuage my self-consciousness created cavities that he was filling. My family would send me here only when I had a toothache. Then we could barely afford the few dollars to pay the dentist, even this one in a rundown building.

Sergei (of course I wouldn't think of addressing him by his first name) smacked his lips before he began a sentence. He told me, regretfully, how much he had left behind in Russia. He painted a picture of an elegant city apartment and a dacha in the country. Then he sighed, looked upward, and said, "But what they did to the Czar's family I at least avoided." I listened intently because I was fascinated, but also to try to understand his words. For an hour-and-a-half he worked on my mouth. My jaws were tired from keeping them wide open, and my ears were tired from trying to understand him.

I left his office and headed for the subway. My mouth was still anesthetized. I was careful not to bite my lip. On the subway platform, I clicked my heels. Out loud I tried to imitate his Russian accent with my numbed mouth. Embarrassed that people were staring at me, I ducked into the nearest subway car.

MY UNDISTINGUISHED ATHLETIC HISTORY

I'm not sure whether my lack of athletic prowess was due to physical weakness or lack of self-confidence that I manifested early in life. When I was nine, boys were chosen for a game of sports. I was often the last one chosen. In the game of stickball my performance as batter and fielder was much less than outstanding.

I excelled in running. Perhaps I learned speed by running away from toughs who wanted to beat me up. I finished first in the 100-yard dash at a school competition at George Wingate Field in Brooklyn. But fame was not to be my fate.

In high school I was chosen for a relay race team. The event took place indoors in a New York City armory. The race began. Two of my teammates had a commanding lead. My heart drummed with anticipation as a runner handed me the baton. I had barely begun my dash when I slipped and spread-eagled on the smooth floor. The embarrassment of losing and the skinned knee were bad enough, but mostly I was contrite for letting my teammates down.

My athletic experiences continued later in life.

In college I took up boxing. To my surprise, I discovered that I had the instinct of a killer. I could beat many competitors by pounding away, including a boy sturdier than me. Maybe I wanted to get even with the boys who had bullied me years earlier. I soon found out that I was not a boxer. When I tried to pound John M, a lanky redhead, he merely stepped back and threw punches at me with his long arms. I was a fighter. He was a boxer. After the bout I sat in my next hour's class, my head bobbing and aching. I had trouble concentrating on the lecture. World War II was upon us. Soon I would have to register for military service. In order to get my choice of the military, I feared that my already poor eyesight would worsen, and so I gave up the gory glory of the ring.

Years later at a graduate school picnic we played touch football. My hands acted as though greased—a football passed to me somehow slipped through my grasp. But even worse, I collided with another player and my eyeglasses cut into my face. My wife took me to a nearby hospital where they stitched the wound. I survived but I shunned touch football, or any football, for that matter.

Even the presumably mild sport of volleyball left me with a sprained ankle and a plaster cast after I jumped up and came down the wrong way.

As an adult many years later I had a tennis-playing woman friend who encouraged me to take up the game. I took a tennis class, taught by a seventeen-year-old who acted like a civilian sergeant, an uncivil one. He taunted me, "You're not holding the racket right. Are you a man or a girl? Get with it!" I developed tennis elbow shortly afterward and gave up the game.

Is it any wonder that I don't play competitive sports and confine myself to hiking?

CONFESSION OF A SOCIABLE LONER

Sounds like an oxymoron, doesn't it? I don't think it is for me...

Being a loner probably began when my family moved frequently from one neighborhood to another. As I mentioned before, I was the new kid on the block, a stranger who could be challenged to a fight, browbeaten or ignored. I went to new schools where the kids knew one another, sometimes for years.

Even as an adult, when I see a large group of boys over twelve, I sometimes feel a sense of distrust.

Mother's need to move to better neighborhoods when finances permitted. The reverse was moving downward when finances looked bleak, as they often did. I would have preferred to remain wherever we were, where I could reach equilibrium with my play- and school-mates, and perhaps develop some friendships that would last more than the year or two. Seven schools were more than enough. But at age six, seven or even thirteen, I had no vote in the matter.

My loneness became a confused loneliness in adolescent years. At fourteen, I was invited to join a group of boys and girls who socialized every weekend, and. I went once or twice, and they encouraged me to join with them. I recall thinking that I didn't want to be pinned down to any one group. I would feel claustrophobic. I didn't realize that I was acting out my past. Yet at the same time I thought irrationally that nobody wanted me, a projection of my own desire to remain aloof.

I hike mostly alone, accompanied by my thoughts, observing wildlife, talking into my recorder when ideas for poems or other writings flow into my mind.

Since I was divorced many years ago, I have lived alone. Of course I had friends and lovers, but most of my time is and has been spent alone in my house, on the trail, and taking care of errands. That's the "loner" part. I enjoy my own presence, my solitude. I can read, write, hike, eat, sleep, and so on.

Well what about the "sociable" part? That intrigues even me. I love to be with people. It's fun to smile and laugh with them, perhaps gently tease. I noticed that during and after a party, or even lunch with a group of people in the class, I often feel "high." The contact triggers something special in me in the presence of others. Still, I used to hike with a group of people, but they move rapidly, and I prefer to smell the proverbial roses. And so mostly I hike alone with my thoughts, observing wildlife, talking into my recorder as ideas for poems or other writings flow into my mind. Even at that, if a friend calls me for a small group hike I usually accept the offer.

I prefer intimate social gatherings, where I have more contact with individuals, rather than larger groups of people .I don't relate easily to the latter, with occasional exceptions.

And so I say that I am a loner, but a sociable one.

RETURN TO OCEAN PARKWAY

More than fifty years! Could it have been that long ago? I visited our old neighborhood. The apartment house we had lived in 363 Ocean Parkway was still there, but my friend Norman's one-family house had been replaced by an apartment house.

I drove closer to Avenue C. My chest pounded, as though I was about to see Marjorie, my long-lost would-be love from junior high school. She lived in a house around the corner. An apartment house has replaced her home, so the search ended there. Instead I slipped into a rare parking place in front of the house I lived in. Cars were few then. But the increased number of cars accompanying increased wealth made finding a parking space challenging.

I walked into the alley that led to the backyard. I looked up to the third floor. There was the window-sill where I did some chemical experiments at home.

Someone left the house. I took advantage of the unlocked door and walked up to the third floor. Was it apartment 3C? I wasn't sure. The grayness of memory dulled the technicolor of the past.

I returned down the stairs and out to the front lawn. I remembered Ratner, the surly janitor in the adjoining apartment house and his equally hostile chow dog. When I was ten, my girl friend Gloria lived in that house. I shrugged my shoulders. Thomas Wolfe wrote, "You can't go home again." Well, you can, but it's no longer the same place. I suppose that's what he meant.

SUMMER DAY ON CONEY ISLAND

It was a clear summer's day in 1940. My friends and I had taken the Brighton Beach Express, and laid down our blankets—our islands in the sand. Many other New Yorkers also abandoned the City's heat to the heat of Coney Island. We depended on the ocean to cool us off. We teased and splashed one another in the Atlantic. But even after emerging from the cool water, our feet burned when we walked a hundred feet to our blanket on the beach. We tickled the feet of our friends who were lying down, their bodies baking in the hot sun. We shoveled sand to cover others who lay back, so they might cool in the sub-surface sand. Our spot was almost literally that—we were surrounded, captive of a million others, all with their own spots.

Hawkers sold ice cream, cold drinks, and soft pretzels, with an eye over the shoulder to avoid the prowling police who carried clubs and other weapons and symbols of their power. Merchants objected to competition with the young men who barely eked a living this way, and didn't have permits that would eat into their meager profits. In pursuit, the police were at a disadvantage in their dark blues and street shoes. Although their prey were dressed for the outdoors, the weight of their wares slowed them down, their pockets jingling with coins, as they tried to outrun the cops. If the police got too close, the sellers often dropped their goods to escape the law's clutches, and kept running. I rooted for the sellers.

Beyond the beach was the famous boardwalk, with legal stores selling food, drinks, and merchandise for tourists. Below the boardwalk, the sands were cold and moist—a place to hide from the sun. The dank smell and the stomping of the walkers above them were mildly unpleasant. Couples were willing to brave these drawbacks to make love, or at least love's preliminaries. They had limited privacy because little boys, wandering away from their mothers, enjoyed interrupting and teasing the lovers.

On the beach were clashing sounds of radios, playing Frank Sinatra or Bing Crosby, accompanied by an obbligato melange of "Get yer ice cream. Get yer ice-cold sodas. Get yer hot pretzels." These calls, between a whisper and a shout, were delicately balanced, loud enough to be heard by potential customers, but not too loud to alert the men in blue.

As late afternoon drew on, we changed to our street clothes. "Make a circle!" one of us shouted in a feigned Yiddish accent. Our friends encircled each of us in turn, holding a large towel or blanket as a privacy screen. We wriggled out of our swim trunks and struggled with our clothing, at times balancing precariously on one leg.

We returned to the train and home, happy, laughing, and teasing. Glowing with sunburn, we resisted being touched.

JEWBASTID

You won't find the word in the dictionary, but at one time it was in my lexicon, through no choice of mine. The pronunciation was typically New Yawk street tawk. Also there was kike, Christ-killer (who me?), mockey. Particularly offensive to me was Jewboy. Much later it would be used as a band's gimmicky name, "Kinky Friedman and the Texas Jewboys." Kinky ran unsuccessfully for governor of Texas years later. But to me the word Jewboy remained offensive.

I mentioned before that kids in a parochial school I passed on my biweekly trip to the library were hostile to Jews. If I stopped and looked through the cyclone fence at their games they shouted "Getatta here, you dirty Jew." Dirty even if I had emerged from a bath recently. I learned that the school was a Polish Catholic one, and that Polish kids (and I suppose their parents) were overtly hostile to my people. My parents experienced pogroms that led them to emigrate to the USA. Betrayal by some Poles during the Jewish uprising in the Polish Ghetto in World War II confirmed their hatred for Jews. Many other Eastern Europeans including Russians similarly hated Jews.

Before she married, my mother had to pretend to be a Christian to get a sales position at Hearn's, a New York department store owned by Catholics. She wore a cross and had to write JMJ on each receipt, for Jesus, Mary and Joseph. Mother could have easily passed, with her blue eyes, blonde hair, small pert nose, and her maiden name of Chasan. Most of the Chasan clan and their spouses seem to have abandoned the trappings of Judaism, although they recognized that gentiles considered them Jews. I think of the composer Mendelssohn, whose parents converted to Christianity so the boy musical genius would have a career. Would he be considered a Jew or not? To Hitler he would be a Jew.

Mother celebrated Christmas in her way, hanging a stocking for me and putting an orange in it. Also she would sing "Silent Night" in German. Her actions were neither clearly Christian nor Jewish. Was it her unspoken wish to be a gentile? Others have labeled this kind of behavior as that of a self-hating Jew. I think that is too strong a word. I would call it a self-denying Jew. She still often used the term *goyim*, the Yiddish word for gentiles, although she had many Christian friends. I think of the inverse of "Some of my best friends are Jews" an old hackneyed phrase implying the speaker is not a bigot.

Many years later I visited her. She had just returned from the A&P grocery store and said that the gentiles looked at her with hatred. I suggested that she was imagining it. "You don't even look Jewish. I never feel any hostile stares at the store," I said.

She insisted, "*They* know."

MOTHER RECONSIDERED

Throughout my memoir I have talked about my ambivalence, in fact dislike of my mother, and how she was so critical of me. Though I didn't think she really loved me, I learned much later that she did. Once years ago as an adult I was deeply depressed. I said to her, "You ruined my life." Of course she was upset, and I regret my words. But much later when I wanted to buy a large country property that I loved and couldn't afford, she unhesitatingly gave me the down payment for it, though she was a city person. It remains a testimony that she never had been able to express her love to me, thinking it would "spoil" me.

AMBIVALENCE

At times in my late teens and early twenties I was asked how I spelled my name. The questioner was often trying to be subtle. I understood that one "n" meant I was Jew, and two "n's" meant that I might possibly be a non-Jewish German. My facial features, my light colored hair and blue-green eyes did not reveal my origin, or at least were ambiguous.

Once on a Friday night, Mike U. said, "Rothman, you going to eat ham for dinner tonight?" asked with an edge to it. Many years late I confronted him. He was surprised and didn't even remember it, but times had changed.

I used to wish I had a real American (WASP) name. White would be good, and Armstrong would be even better, thinking of Jack Armstrong on the radio, the All-American Boy. After college I considered denying my Jewish identity to change my name to Redman, a direct translation of Rothman, perhaps acting out mother's ambivalence or self-rejection as a Jew. My denial persisted until after World War II. Though never an observant one, my self-identity is definitely as a Jew.

XIV. CONCLUSION

After my long diversions, I return to my post-graduate year in high school. In my spare time at Stuyvesant I studied for the Aptitude and Achievement Tests required for entrance to Columbia and many other colleges and universities.

I hopped the subway to the grand New York Public Library in midtown Manhattan. It was early winter and snow covered the streets. The air was nippy, but I spent most of my time indoors in the library. I read over old exams, trying to expand my already adequate vocabulary, and reviewing mathematics problems. I became bleary-eyed after a few hours of this deadly stuff, but I persisted.

I stopped for dinner and hurried over to Horn & Hardart's Automat Cafeteria, to have a quick meal before returning to the library. Foods were displayed through glass doors and placed on shelves that could be rotated remotely to make one's choice, reminding me of the revolving entry doors in prominent hotels. I put my nickels and dimes in slots. The automatic glass doors swung upward, presenting the food. A gourmand, I loved the well done, almost dried out baked beans that a gourmet would reject. Their rich scent and warm taste filled me with pleasure, enhanced by my hunger. I ended the meal with a glass of milk. Sadly, the Automat is no more. I wish it had been saved as a historical site.

I returned to 42nd street. The streets were darker and slippery. I pulled up my coat collar to shield my neck, and leaned against the cold wind, trying to remain upright on the icy sidewalk. I returned to the library and studied until the library closed at ten PM.

It was time to write letters to colleges, seeking scholarship assistance. I was accepted at Wagner, a Lutheran College on nearby Staten Island. Brooklyn Polytechnic Institute turned me down. Years later I attended classes at night while employed and received a Master's degree from Poly. I could have qualified for Cooper Union or City College of New York, but my real desire was Columbia College, the men's undergraduate college of Columbia University. I contacted Columbia and applied for a scholarship. I impatiently awaited the results of my application. I longed to attend this prestigious university, but my family certainly couldn't afford the $400 yearly tuition, a princely sum at the time, plus books and incidentals. Instead I probably would have had to attend a free institution like City College or Cooper Union. I applied for scholarships to other universities. Harvard offered me a tuition scholarship, but the funding was insufficient to cover the additional cost of room and board.

I became restless and decided to work gainfully, while waiting to hear from Columbia. I learned from the classified ads that the starting salary of apprentice machinists was sixteen dollars a week. Our high school required us to take various shops as well as the usual academic and scientific subjects, and so I could have easily qualified as a beginning machinist.

On my lunch hour I went to an employment agency. An agent met me at the door. His first question was "What is your nationality?" I understood the import of his question. Without thinking, I said, "Jewish."

"Sorry, no openings."

The answer he needed to hear for me to be hired was Christian or American, a disguised word for Christian.

It was 1941. War was in the air and was taking place in Europe. The US was building for war, and there was much activity in the defense industry. But not for Jews. Only years later did I realize that I could have responded truthfully, that my nationality was American. Instead of the response expected by the interviewer, I should have forced him to probe further, and he probably would have. But at seventeen I was naïve and defensive about being Jewish. The interviewer might have been Jewish himself, working under constraints placed on him by potential employers, whose ultimate funding, ironically, came from the US government.

HOBAR AND TWINFACE

Instead, I found a job in Manhattan at Hobar Sales Company, its name a contraction of those of its partners— Hochheimer and Baril. William Hochheimer was a tall, slender, pleasant-speaking man. Samuel Baril, was a bald, roly-poly man with thick fingers and a direct, almost challenging manner. Hochheimer was Protestant and Baril, Jewish. They apparently had no problem with their religious difference and didn't discriminate in hiring.

A group of us assembled Twinface clocks, which had a face on the front and on the back of the clock. A single set of gears drove the hands so they read the same time on both faces. These upscale items offered a choice of pigskin or Florentine leather cases among others. They were sold to Hammacher-Schlemmer, Neiman-Marcus, and other hyphenated, expensive stores. We inserted gears in the clocks and placed them on a shelf at various stages of completion. The problem was keeping them running. At least half of them were stoppers, the word we used for the intransigent ones. Some gave up a within a day. The more frustrating ones waited up to a week later. By then we had enclosed the clockwork in their leather cases and had to dismantle and troubleshoot them. We constantly took them apart and put them together, shaving metal where we thought they hung up. The clocks kept defeating our attempts to repair them—the Revolt of the Inanimate. Baril and Hochheimer were understandably concerned. Baril said, "We must routinize our work." Routinize? Tell that to the stubborn clocks.

The workers at Hobar were Jews or gentiles. Joe was Catholic, and there were two Jewish Reubens. The elder was a handsome man of twenty-some years, with dark curly hair and a go-go spirit. Jo, the secretary, a pretty, delicately textured Irish-American young woman, was clearly attracted to the handsome one. Rueben seemed impervious to her obvious interest in him. Another woman was curvaceous Esther, a Jewish woman who assembled other Hobar products like silk-covered clothes hangers. She wore slippers and was always dressed casually, as though lounging in her home. In my adolescent hormonal years, I had sexual fantasies about her. She seemed dressed for bed.

To overcome the boredom and frustration of our task, we clock-assemblers indulged in ironic humor. When not in earshot of the bosses, we sang songs popular at the time like "I'll Never Smile Again," substituting words like "They'll never run again." We clockers engaged in constant banter. When the younger Reuben working on a repair asked for a knife, handsome Reuben said, "Take it out of my back." We had only a few jokes, but they were repeated often, like mantras.

We were unhappy with our pay—ten dollars a week, the Federal minimum at the time. We complained to one other about it. Handsome Reuben as a senior employee was paid a few bucks more than the minimum. Nevertheless, he approached the boss about salaries. Sam Baril hit the ceiling, snarling words like "trouble-makers, communists," his angry response. "You better not plan to unionize!"

We gave up. About then, thanks to the Roosevelt administration, the legal minimum was raised to twelve dollars a week.

Once more I tried for a machinist position at a different employment agency. Again I was rebuffed for the same reason as before.

I retreated to my job at Twinface.

While sitting in nearby Bryant Park during my lunch hours, I read the Durants' *History of Philosophy*, that served as an antidote to the routine work of assembling clocks.

EXAM TIME

On a rainy Saturday I took the full day scholarship examinations—the aptitude test int the morning and the achievement test in the afternoon. Certain that I did poorly on the latter test, I returned home with an unaccustomed throbbing headache. Mother asked, "How did you do?"

I growled, "I don't want to talk about it." I was certain that I failed to get good grades in Latin, and my prospects for a Columbia scholarship seemed bleak.

Frank Bowles, the Admissions Officer at Columbia had previously interviewed me. At least I got that far. Then I waited a few interminable months to hear from the College.

I continued to work with the clocks. I developed a heart pain that worried me. Mother brought me to Dr. Chinn, an African-American physician. The diagnosis was that I had been swallowing air that pressed against my heart. Dr Chinn said it was not serious and was probably caused by my stress waiting to hear from Columbia.

One day a letter arrived from Columbia. I held my breath, anticipating a rejection. Instead, I had won one of the ten Pulitzer tuition scholarships to Columbia College awarded to graduates of New York City high schools. Two of the ten were won by Stuyvesant High, one of fifty eligible high schools in the City. In addition we were given $250 dollars for each of four years for books and incidentals, a considerable sum at the time.

Wow! Fireworks! Double rainbows!!

Brooklyn was in my past, Twinface was in my past, and Columbia was to be in my future. I moved with my family to Manhattan. Before I was a visitor. Now I have crossed the bridge and become a resident Manhattanite, and a soon-to-be real Columbian. A happy ending and a new beginning.

About the Author

Albert Rothman was born in Brooklyn, NY in 1924, and attended Stuyvesant High School in New York City. He was awarded a Pulitzer Scholarship to Columbia University where he received a BS in1944. Polytechnic University awarded him a Masters degree in 1951, and the University of California at Berkeley a PhD in chemistry and chemical engineering in 1954. He has lived in the San Francisco Bay Area since 1948.

He is an avid hiker, a source for his nature poetry and prose and for his adventures. He is a long-time classical music lover and collector.

Retired in 1986 after a varied career in chemical research, he traveled extensively and is working on a forthcoming memoir about his ten-week camping journey, where he hiked all the western national parks. Since retirement, he has written and published many personal essays, memoirs, poems, short stories, and political letters.

He belongs to several writers' groups including the California Writers Club and the Ina Coolbrith Poetry Circle.

He received first and several other prizes in Ina Coolbrith Circle poetry contests, and a first prize in a Marguerite A. Sousa Poetry Competition, published in The Poets' Edge Magazine. He has received many awards for his writings and publication in the annual Las Positas College Anthology every year since 1996. Other poems and prose pieces have appeared in the Northwoods Journal, the Dan River Anthology, New Horizons, and other anthologies. He has presented some of his prose and poems at coffee houses and other venues.

Acknowledgments

I am indebted to Nancy O'Connell. I began to write episodes about my past in her class. Nancy encouraged me to bring the pieces together in a book about my Brooklyn boyhood. Nancy also did an early editing of my manuscript.

I want to thank Beth Brewster who urged me to enroll in Nancy's class years ago.

David Wright's class at Las Positas College was my first ongoing class in writing, where I began to write short stories. He liked my work and encouraged me to submit my stories for publication. He continues to be a valued friend.

Thanks also to Penny Warner for a group writing class at her home several years ago.

My close and dear friend Helen Daniel has been supportive of my work and kindly did a second editing of my manuscript.

Elisabeth Tuck, a professional editor did a final detailed editing with excellent suggestions to improve the text. I consider her an outstanding editor. Any leftover mistakes are mine, since I added more bits to my manuscript.

Postscript

I am fortunate. Many have given me reason to enjoy the life I had and have. Dad's loving acceptance and Mother's emphasis on academics helped me succeed. She also helped instill in me the love of music that she transmitted. The teachers who introduced me to music and nature. Joseph Pulitzer who endowed scholarships for New York City boys to Columbia, one of which I was fortunate to obtain. My relatives who gave me a broad base of affection and belonging. Finally the freedom my parents gave me to wander on Brooklyn streets that taught me a self-reliance and adventurousness. All have contributed to my life.

LaVergne, TN USA
26 July 2010
190997LV00001B/18/P